VICKI COURTNEY

YourBoy

Raising a Godly Son in an Ungodly World

B&H
PUBLISHING GROUP

NASHVILLE, TENNESSEE

ISBN: 978-1-4336-7693-2

Published by B&H Publishing Group,
Nashville, Tennessee

Dewey Decimal Classification: 306.874
Subject Heading: MOTHERS AND SONS \
VIRTUE \ BOYS

Unless otherwise noted, Scripture quotations are from the
Holy Bible, New International Version, copyright
© 1973, 1978, 1984 by International Bible Society. Other ver-
sions include: HCSB, Holman Christian Standard Bible® ©
1999, 2000, 2002, 2003 by Holman Bible Publishers; NRSV,
New Revised Standard Version, copyright 1989 by
the Division of Christian Education of the National Council of
Churches of Christ in the United States of America,
used by permission, all rights reserved; NLT, New Living
Translation, copyright © 1996. Used by permission of Tyndale
House Publishers, Inc., Wheaton, Illinois 60189.
All rights reserved; NKJV, New King James Version, copyright ©
1979, 1980, 1982, Thomas Nelson, Inc., Publishers; and KJV,
King James Version.

1 2 3 4 5 6 7 8 • 16 15 14 13 12

Dedication

To my sons, Ryan and Hayden . . .
A mother could not ask for two finer boys. It has been a honor and privilege to cheer you on your journey to manhood. I can't wait to see what God has in store for you!

Contents

Introduction

For me, the reality of motherhood did not come during pregnancy. Nor did it come with the "It's a boy" announcement in the delivery room. The reality of motherhood came hours later when a nurse entered my room holding a freshly bathed and swaddled infant and said "Mrs. Courtney, your *son* is ready to see you." *My son. I had a son.* Her words somehow made motherhood official—more than the positive result on the pregnancy test, more than the countless baby showers, more than hearing the heartbeat for the first time or even feeling the first kick. When the nurse tucked my sleeping son into the crook of my arm with his tiny head resting on my beating heart, I could hardly breathe. I had carried this precious bundle for nine months, and now, for the first time since his grand entry into the world, we were alone. Just the two of us. Mother and son. I felt certain my heart would explode at any moment, unable to contain the love I felt for this child. It was a brand of love I had never experienced before.

The following day when my husband and I were preparing to leave the hospital, I almost expected the nurse to return with an announcement that the baby would have to stay. My husband later confessed to feeling the same way. We were so young and inexperienced! Didn't we have to take some kind of test or something before we could leave the hospital and be trusted with such an awesome responsibility? For heaven's sakes, I had to jump through more hoops to get a library card! The feelings of inadequacy would follow me home. *Did I have what it takes*

1

to be a mother? And not just a mother, but a good mother? In the years that followed, the same questions would resurface from time to time, but they were over-shadowed by my trust in God, the ultimate loving Parent. *"You can do this,"* He would remind me in the silent places of my heart.

Veteran moms would encourage and remind me along the way, "Enjoy it! It goes by so fast." And yet, while time seemed to stand still in those early years, there were sobering reminders along the way that the clock was ticking. There was the first day of kindergarten when I dropped my son, Ryan, off at the door to his classroom. The teacher welcomed him and closed the door behind us as the bell rang. I was distracted by my three-year-old daughter who was hanging onto my leg and begging for a "bicket from MyDonald's" (translation: a biscuit from McDonald's) and a five-month-old who was fussing to get out of his carrier. Somehow, I sensed that it was a sacred, defining moment of sorts and stood motionless in the hallway. As I looked through the rectangular pane of glass in the door, I could see the students seated in a semi-circle, their eyes intent on what their new teacher was saying. I waited for Ryan to turn back so I could give him a reassuring smile and wave. He never did. Of course, I cried all the way to McDonald's.

Then there was the seventh grade flag football game where he broke away from the pack on the last play of the game and ran 85 yards for a winning touchdown. I ran the entire length of the field along the sidelines, cheering him on all the way. After the game, I was strictly instructed to make sure it never happened again. He didn't seem to mind my cheering before, but suddenly, almost overnight, my *encouragement* had evolved into *embarrassment*. A year later, while chaperoning a school dance, I would be reminded again of the fleeting time when I watched my son slow dance for the first time. Worse over, he had the nerve to actually enjoy it! Yes, I was slowly losing my boy.

Today that baby boy is six feet tall and months shy of walking across the stage at graduation. He is a proud member of the "Class of 2006." While I expect to shed a few tears on graduation day, I am preparing myself for a day that will follow shortly thereafter—the day his dad and I will drop him off at college. And if you think for a minute that it is of some consolation that I will still have his younger brother (aka: "the baby") at home for five more years, think again. When I dropped Hayden (my youngest of three children) off on the first day of kindergarten, some of the other moms who were dropping off their "babies" headed to Starbucks for a round of celebratory lattes to toast their newfound freedom. Not me. I sat in my car and cried my eyes out for thirty minutes as I mourned the realization that a phase of my life was forever over. No more impromptu afternoon picnics or hikes to the fishing pond behind our house while his older brother and sister were at school. Over. Gone. And onto a new chapter.

Today my little fisherman is a seventh grader who dons a shaggy doo, plays the electric guitar, obsesses over sports, and gets his house wrapped by a group of giggly girls on a regular basis. I can't even bring myself to volunteer to chaperone at his school dances. They would have to have to cart me off on a gurney when the first slow song played. I am all too aware that each and every milestone achieved in the "baby's" life marks the closure of a chapter in *my* life.

Fast forward to today: 2012 (six years later)

I penned the words above in the original introduction for this book back in 2006. When my editor asked me to write an updated introduction, I welcomed the opportunity, because a lot has happened in six years! As I reflected back on my sons' milestones in the original introduction above, I couldn't help but note the irony of the timing of writing this updated introduction. I mentioned the conflict of emotion that comes with "closing a chapter," and I've closed quite a few chapters in this past year alone. That seventh grader (aka: "the baby") with the shaggy doo, moved into a college dorm to begin his freshman year. He is involved in a weekly Bible study, Young Life leadership, and has found a wonderful posse of friends who love Jesus. The closing of that chapter signaled the opening of a new one called "the empty nest years." I informed my husband that this milestone also merits a chapter called "vacation on a white sand beach," which we are in the process of planning.

And what about my oldest boy, who was just months shy of graduating high school when I wrote the original introduction? He graduated last year from Auburn University, relocated back to his hometown of Austin to take a job (thank you, Jesus!), and he is married to an amazing Christian girl. But, here's the best part: they have a new baby boy! (Yes, that officially makes me a GRANDMA! Perhaps, my next book should be *Your GRANDboy!*) Ryan has stepped up to the plate when it comes to being a godly husband and father. In addition to being involved in a weekly Bible study and a weekly accountability group, he and his wife Casey, attend our home church.

Both of my boys are in a sweet place with the Lord and I couldn't be more proud (and relieved?!). But here's what I need you to know: The journey to get to this sweet place wasn't without bumps along the way. There were times along the way when my boys strayed from God's path to sample the world's offerings. There were even some times when my husband and I wondered if our efforts to help build a foundation of faith in their lives would ever pay off. We persevered during the tough times and stayed engaged in their lives. We continued to monitor their peer group, their technology, and hold fast to rules and boundaries that would help safeguard their hearts. Most importantly, we continued to point them to the cross of Christ and confidently remind them that the world's offerings pale in comparison to His unfailing love. And of course, we prayed. And prayed. And prayed.

As mothers, we have been given a task to grow the next generation of godly men, and I believe it is one of the highest callings in a mother's life. We have been given a brief eighteen years to make a godly impact on our sons. Eighteen years to teach them about the God we serve. Eighteen years to impress God's commandments upon their hearts. Eighteen years to train them to be "real men" living in the real world. Eighteen years to influence them in a way their fathers cannot. Eighteen years to be the #1 gal in their lives. And eighteen years to ready ourselves for that day when we must release them to a waiting world. Let us remember that our sons, while they will always be "our boys," belong first and foremost to Him.

Part 1

IT'S A BOY!

CHAPTER 1

Snips, Snails, and Puppy Dog Tails

A man loves his sweetheart the most,
his wife the best, but his mother the longest.
—IRISH PROVERB

Before I had children, I was one of those women who absolutely had to have a girl. If I had to have a dozen kids to get that girl, so be it. When I found out I was expecting my first child, I had visions of pink smocked dresses, dainty hair bows, play kitchens, dress-up clothes, ballet lessons, and all the other standard female accoutrements. It's not that I didn't want a boy; I just couldn't picture myself with a boy. And so for nine months I waited for the verdict.

This was long before you could get an ultrasound on a routine doctor's visit. Mothers today have more video footage of their babies before they ever take a breath than I have of my entire childhood. I have young mother friends who start scrapbooking before the baby has a heartbeat.

I had no such luxury, so I had no choice but to wait and wait and wait. No worries, though, because according to the old wives' tales, I was having a girl. I carried the baby high, the heartbeat was fast, and I craved sweets. Who needs an ultrasound with that kind of foolproof evidence? And so I continued to think pink. All the way up until the final push, my mind was filled with thoughts of the daughter I had always dreamed of. OK, so I lied. Actually, at that moment my mind was filled with thoughts like: *This is the most excruciating pain I have ever felt in my entire life. Forget my dream of three or four children. This kid is going to be an only child!*

I did, however, have one tiny clue just moments before the baby's birth that prepared me for the fact that I just might not have a girl. As my baby was entering the world, a nurse in the delivery room said, "Wow! Look at the shoulders on that football player!"

Football player? I thought. *Great, if it is a girl, she's going to look like Helga the Amazon queen.* And with that sobering thought, I was almost relieved to hear the "It's a boy!" announcement.

Within minutes my baby boy was cleaned up, wrapped in a blanket, and handed over to me for inspection. Funny thing, not once in those first moments of holding my new son did I wish he had been a girl.

In those early years I experienced firsthand the indescribable bond God creates between a mother and her son. Sure, many of us are blessed with husbands who do a pretty good job in the unconditional love department, but a son, especially in those early years, will melt your heart with his shameless adoration. What mother cannot remember in detail the priceless things her boys say to her in those years? "Mom, when I grow up, I'm going to marry you." "Mom, you are bootiful." "Mom, I love you infinite times infinite times a thousand." Or, as my second son, Hayden, said to me at the age of six when he crawled up in my lap to snuggle, "Mom, you are my kind of woman." Perhaps that is what makes the mother-son bond so different from the mother-daughter bond. Mom is truly the number one woman in her son's life in the early years. She is the reigning queen of his heart.

Our sons' unconditional love and adoration help quell any leftover residue of pain we may have suffered at the hands of countless other boys in those awkward growing-up years. Remember when we obsessed over whether the boys thought we were pretty? Well, guess what? Our sons think we are—sans the makeup and with an extra twenty pounds! Remember sweating it out wondering if we would get asked to the home-coming dance? This boy will dance to our heart's content and turn the average kitchen into an elegant ballroom. Remember waiting by the phone, hoping that special boy would call? This boy will call you nonstop on his pretend phone! Our sons will place us on a pedestal that ascends into the starry heights of heaven. One look into their adoring eyes and we are forever hooked. Yet, in the back of our minds, we know it cannot last forever. Eventually another woman will become the object of their affections. As mothers it is our job to nurture and prepare our sons for that day.

We will always hold a special and unique place in our sons' hearts even though their outward displays of love will lessen as the years go on. Don't you love when the camera cuts to the fans during a televised football game? You can almost always count on seeing a grown son with a "Hi, Mom!" sign in the crowd.

My older son is months shy of flying the nest as I write this book, and I can honestly say I have had a blast with him. I am not a perfect parent; I have made many mistakes along the way. Fortunately love covers a multitude of sins (1 Pet. 4:8). If given the opportunity to do it over, I can think of many things I would do differently, but I honestly can't imagine the outcome being any better. I am so proud of the young man he has become—in spite of my parenting mistakes along the way.

I treasure the relationship I have with my boys. Even though the "coolness factor" has set in and I have reached official dork status, there are still moments when they will surprise me and melt my heart all over again. My older son was never much of a snuggler in the early years, but today this six-foot-tall strapping young man will put his arm around me and tell me out of the blue, "Mom, I love you." And get this—he will do this in public! In his middle school years, he wouldn't have dared to risk such a move. He had to prove that he wasn't a mama's boy as he journeyed into manhood.

I am a mother in the trenches just like you, and I've had my share of blood, sweat, and tears along the way to prove it. I've done plenty of things wrong, and I've done plenty of things right. But, if I could give you one word of advice as a mother who has a son about to head off to college, it would be to enjoy every stage of your son's journey to manhood. When older mothers, such as myself, come along and remind you of how fast time with your son passes, take heed. It's so very true. We only have our sons for a little while, so let's make the best of the time God has given us. Raising a godly son in an ungodly world is not an easy task, but it is an eternally rewarding one.

Before we dive in and tackle the subject of raising a godly son in an ungodly world, let's brush up on some basic truths that, if not understood, can hinder our noble efforts. Where do you stand in regard to the following truths?

There Is No Such Thing as a Perfect Mother

Admit it. At some point you have crossed paths with supermom and have felt less than adequate. You know her—she started the phonics tapes when her child was *in utero*, documents every momentous occasion, including first breath, first tear, first tooth, first haircut, first tantrum, first time-out, and first everything-that-follows, with volumes of scrapbooks. Her kids' socks are whiter than other kids' socks, and their lunches include something from each of the four food groups. Every item of clothing they own is initialed or monogrammed and has a clean fresh smell. Her kids are well groomed, polite, and say "nice to meet you" on cue while your kids duke it out on the front lawn and scream "shut up" and "stupid" loud enough for everyone within a two-mile radius to hear. Her children never have snotty noses, belch in public, or wear their shoes on the wrong feet. You can't remember the last time your kids even *wore* shoes.

Supermom's house is sparkling clean and always sports a piney fresh scent. She is PTA president, drives on every field trip, and still has time for the gym. She has enough energy at the end of the day to make one wonder if she is doing espresso shots every couple of hours. She is the mom we love to hate (unless you *are* her!). Her sheer presence serves as a reminder that no matter how hard we try, we will never be *her*.

The truth is, even supermom is not without her flaws. In reality, there are probably some things about you that she longs to have. Besides, supermom may not be the best-suited mom for *your* kids. I learned this lesson many years ago when one of my children spent the night with a friend whose mom had made it on my list of supermoms. Days later my child made a comment about not wanting to go back to this friend's house because supermom "was mean and screamed all the time." So, you see, supermoms are not perfect.

There is only one standard by which we should measure ourselves, and that is up against the parent God has called us to be. He knows we will make mistakes along the way, but he is full of patience, mercy, and grace. I am reminded of Philippians 1:6, which says, "He who began a good work in you will carry it on to completion until the day of Christ Jesus." Tuck that Scripture away in your heart as you read through this book. It would be easy to get overwhelmed with the challenge at hand to raise our boys to be godly in an ungodly world. There is always room for improvement, but the truth is, you are a super-mom, or you wouldn't have picked up this book.

There Is No Such Thing as a Perfect Child

I don't care if you have read every Christian parenting book on the market and taken every parenting workshop imaginable—it is not a matter of *if* your kids will disappoint you and break your heart but *when*. Take it from someone who has read multitudes of Christian parenting books, taken and taught Christian parenting workshops, and even written books on parenting—no one is exempt.

I learned this not long ago when I awoke in the middle of the night and went downstairs to get a drink. In doing so, I noticed the door to my office was closed. As I approached the door, I heard my older son talking softly on the phone. I stood outside the door and listened as he confessed to this friend to trying alcohol over the summer and get this—with several other "good, Christian friends" whom he implicated by name over the phone. I felt as if the wind had been knocked out of me. This is a child that I have called "my little Daniel" for years due to his ability to take a stand for his faith. He is active in youth group, goes on mission trips, is an officer in Fellowship of Christian Athletes, attends a weekly Bible study, and is discipled regularly by his father. Kids like that have no reason to experiment with alcohol; they are exempt from such standard worldly temptations, right? Wrong!

Once I confronted him with my newfound knowledge, he came clean and expressed a sincere repentance. Of course, I beat myself up in the days that followed, convinced that I had apparently not read enough parenting books or taken enough courses to head off such teenage rebellion. About a week later I asked him why he had done it. He basically said it boiled down to nothing more than sheer curiosity. He went on to say, "Mom, I have been good all my life, and I just wondered what it was like."

At that very moment, it hit me—I had somehow imagined that my children would never stray from the path of God. Older, wiser parents had warned me along the way that no amount of books read or hours logged in parenting classes would exempt me from the painful reality that all children have a mind of their own and will not always make choices that reflect the training they have received from their parents. And so, as I stared into the eyes of my teenage boy that day, I saw him in a different light. He is still my "little Daniel," but he is also a *sinner.* A sinner, mind you, just like me. Imagine that. Perhaps, on the upside, he now recognizes his desperate need for a Savior.

Maybe your son is young, and it's hard for you to imagine a day when he will stray from God's path. How can this same little boy, who boldly tells strangers that Jesus is his "very bestest friend" and makes crosses out of Popsicle sticks in Sunday school, grow up and make the choice to *sin?* I certainly don't want to rain on your parade, but let me ask you: "Have you ever strayed from God's path? At the time, did you sincerely love Jesus?" I thought so. We will always battle our sinful natures, and our sons are no different. Try as we may, we cannot make our sons love God and abide by his will in every instance. They possess the same free will that we do, and they will have to come to a place where they choose to use that free will to obey God.

There Is Such a Thing as a Perfect God

If you are like me, you would do anything to protect your son from harm twenty-four hours a day, seven days a week. If only it were possible! I can still recall the first time I left my oldest son, Ryan, with a sitter. I was one of those neurotic mothers who imagined the worst-case scenario in every situation. He was around nine months old, and I must have called home every fifteen minutes to make sure things were running smoothly. Of course, I calmed down by the time I had my third child. By that point the sitter was calling me to see if I was ever coming home.

A mother never really loses that innate sense to hover over her chicks and try to protect them from the dangers and uncertainties of life. The same out-of-control feeling I felt the first time I left Ryan with a sitter returned in full force the first time he walked out the front door with car keys in hand. I have never felt so utterly out of control. Or how about a few weeks later when he started driving to school with his fourteen-year-old sister in tow? And to think that I worried when he zipped around the driveway at the age of two cutting sharp corners until his plastic little coupe car was tipping on the outside two wheels! Now he maneuvers two tons of metal on the open roads with my daughter by his side!

If our sons' physical well-being is not enough to worry about, there are other issues that leave the average mother feeling out of control: online dangers; breakups and broken hearts; failure to make the A team; friends who turn wild; parties that are not adequately chaperoned; a sex-obsessed culture that bombards them relentlessly with a "just-do-it" message day in and day out; invitations to cheat, drink alcohol, and do drugs; and the list goes on and on. Nothing could prepare me for the tug-of-war my heart felt when my son got his license and, thus, gained more freedom. Could I really let go? I had no choice; I had to. Oh sure, he has a curfew, but it's the time in between where I am left wondering if he is safe, if he is where he says he will be, and if he is making wise choices. Fortunately, in the midst of it all, God is there. While I cannot hover over him and watch him every minute of every day, God can and does.

I am reminded of the account of Hannah and her son, Samuel, in 1 Samuel 1:11–28. Barren for many years, Hannah cried out to God for a son and vowed to give him over to God, should God meet her request. God did bless her with a son, and true to her word, Hannah cared for Samuel until he was weaned and then brought him to Eli, the priest, to live out the remainder of his childhood years with Eli at the temple.

After he was weaned, she took the boy with her, young as he was, along with a three-year-old bull, an ephah of flour and a skin of wine, and brought him to the house of the LORD at Shiloh. When they had slaughtered the bull, they brought the boy to Eli, and she said to him, "As surely as you live, my lord, I am the woman who stood here beside you praying to the LORD. I prayed for this child, and the LORD has granted me what I asked of him. So now I give him to the LORD. For his whole life he will be given over to the LORD." And he worshiped the LORD there. (1 Sam. 1:24–28)

What mother could take a child she had nursed at her breast, swayed to sleep in her arms, and watched take his first wobbly steps, and put him in the care of a stranger for the remainder of his childhood years? Only a woman desperately dependent on God. After turning Samuel over to Eli, Hannah made a statement that gives us great insight into her walk with God:

Then Hannah prayed and said: "My heart rejoices in the LORD." (1 Sam. 2:1)

Personally, if I were in her situation, I think I'd be curled up in the fetal position sobbing my eyes out. Hannah, however, was rejoicing in God! Dear mothers, let us pay close heed to Hannah's example. Our sons belong first and foremost to the Lord. He has entrusted each of them into our care for a short time.

Even though Samuel was given over to the Lord, he was not exempt from ungodly influences while in the care of Eli. Scripture tells us that Eli's sons were guilty of treating the Lord's offerings brought by the Israelites with contempt and sleeping with the women who served at the entrance of the Tent of Meeting. Ironically, Samuel would eventually deliver the Lord's spoken judgment against the house of Eli.

As my sons have gotten older and become more exposed to ungodly influences outside of my care and control, I have had to mentally turn them over to the Lord as an act of my will. Hannah was able to follow through with her vow to commit her son to the care of the Lord because she had come to desperately depend on God prior to Samuel's birth. When Hannah was barren, we are told that she "poured out" her soul to the Lord (1 Sam. 1:15). The original Hebrew word used for "poured out" is *shaphak*, which means to "spill forth" or "sprawl out." Hannah was in the habit of depending on God long before she had children. Because of her dependence, Hannah knew better than to think Samuel belonged to her.

And so, as mothers, we rest in the settled peace that our sons are always under the watchful eye of the one perfect parent, God. In the meantime, we have a responsibility to help equip them with the tools needed to be godly in the ungodly world in which they live. What they choose to do with those tools will, of course, be their decision.

CHAPTER 2

Roll Call: Is Dad Present, Absent, or Both?

In all my efforts to learn to read, my mother shared fully
my ambition and sympathized with me and aided mein every
way she could. If I have done anything in life worth attention,
I feel sure that I inherited the disposition from my mother.
—BOOKER T. WASHINGTON

Several years ago, while boarding a plane en route to a speaking engagement, I had an experience that will remain forever etched into my mind. I sat down in my assigned seat in the middle of the row next to a young boy sitting by the window. His back was to me as he stared intently out the window, watching the bags being loaded onto the plane. When the plane was preparing for takeoff, he was still staring out the window, but I noticed that every minute or so, his little shoulders would tremble, and I would hear a sniffle or two. He was crying!

My mother's heart kicked in, and I dug in my purse, praying for a piece of gum to satisfy this divine appointment. Within seconds I had located one, and I leaned over and said, "Sweetie, we're about to take off. Would you like this piece of gum so your ears won't pop?" It proved to be a successful distraction, and as he took the gum, he muttered a faint "thank you" in between his muffled sobs. Before he could turn again to the window to hide his tears, I went for distraction number two. "Hey, I noticed you have a GameBoy there. Do you know how to play Pokemon Yellow?" He looked at me and replied, "I have it in my backpack. I'm real good at it." Bingo—I had myself a new friend.

By the end of the flight, I knew his name and that he was the same age as my younger son, who at the time was eight years old. I also knew that he was traveling to see his dad in another state.

When I asked him if he was excited, he simply replied, "Not really. I didn't want to go, but my mom is making me cuz I have to go see my dad once a year." He then went on to tell me that his dad had a new baby and other kids in his "new family." After playing a couple of games on GameBoy with him and making his list of trusted friends, he shared that he didn't really know his dad and didn't think his dad liked him.

At this point the plane was descending, and I was about to arrive at my destination. He would stay on the plane for the final leg of his trip. In what little time I had, I shared that I thought he was a really special boy and that he had a Father in heaven who absolutely adored him. I told him that when he felt sad, scared, unloved, or alone to remember his Father in heaven would always be there and willing to listen.

It was the second time he smiled during the trip (the first smile came when he thoroughly beat me in GameBoy). It was so hard to leave my new friend. Part of me wanted to stay on that plane and travel the last leg of the trip to meet his good ol' dad. I would have loved the opportunity to tell him what he was missing by not having a relationship with his son. Eight-year-old boys are not supposed to get on airplanes and travel across the country to see their dads. Eight-year-old boys are supposed to shoot hoops in the driveway with their dads, go fishing with their dads, and say bedtime prayers with their dads. And most importantly, eight-year-old boys should have dads they can go to when they are feeling scared, worried, or sad—not dads they are *scared*, *worried*, and *sad* about seeing.

I am extremely grateful that my boys are blessed with a dad who takes his role as father very seriously. We are on the same page as a unified team when it comes to trying to raise our sons to be godly. Because we share the same goals, the truths presented in this book are doubly enforced. My husband is committed to sharing in the physical, spiritual, and emotional training of our children. He takes the time to involve the boys in many household projects, train them in yard work, disciple them, pray with them, and spend one-on-one time with them. He is a significant part of the equation when it comes to raising our boys to be godly young men. Please know that while I present truths and areas of training in this book that are critical in the raising of your sons, I am in no way expecting that one parent could do it all. Keep this in mind as you read along; and depending on your personal situation, feel free to adapt application of these truths to fit the parenting style of your husband and you.

When it comes to raising our sons to be godly, it certainly helps if their dads are fully engaged in the process. However, I know this is not the case in many households. Moms who do not have spouses who are fully engaged in the parenting process may feel overwhelmed when trying to implement many of the truths contained in this book. If you are one of these moms, do not be dismayed; your efforts to raise your sons to be godly will bear fruit. Depending on your situation, here are some things to consider:

If Your Son's Father Is Absent

The encounter with my new friend reminded me of the sobering reality that many boys (and girls) are without their biological fathers in the home. In fact, a whopping 40 percent of children go to bed each night without their biological fathers living in their home to tuck them in. While the absence of a father in the home can have a devastating impact on girls, the absence will be hardest felt for boys who need a male role model to assist them as they journey on the road to manhood. If this is the situation in your home, let me commend you for picking up this book. Clearly you are a caring mother who desires to pass the torch of godliness down to your son(s). Though it is God's ideal for your son to have his biological father in the home and living as a godly role model, it is not a hopeless situation if this is not the case in your home. Trying to apply the truths presented in this book may seem overwhelming to a single mother who alone carries the burden of raising her son(s) to be godly. Regardless, with your effort and his heavenly Father's help, it can be done. Here are some things to consider if you are a single mother or a widow trying to raise your son alone:

- Consider asking a godly male relative or close family friend who lives nearby to occasionally spend one-on-one time with your son. Whether it is a visit to a fast-food restaurant, an overnight campout, or watching a football game together, your son will benefit from being around a positive male role model.

- Consider involving your son in Boy Scouts or a like-minded organization that would help train him in areas where you may be deficient. In the book *Raising a Modern Day Knight*, author Robert Lewis states that "boys become men in the community of men. There is no substitute for this vital component. . . . If your boy is to become a man, you must enlist the community." The word *enlist* implies action. It will take effort on your part to find a positive male community to influence your son, but it is a critical component in his journey to manhood.

- When your son is old enough to understand his loss of a male role model in the home, openly acknowledge the void he must feel. If the loss is due to a negligent father, avoid speaking harsh words against his father. An occasional "I'm sorry your father is not here to take you on the father-son church campout" will keep the lines of communication open. There is no sense in dancing around the issue and pretending it's not a big deal that dad's not around. It *is* a big deal. However, it is also important that you not dwell on it by constantly bringing it up. Bring it up when you feel that your son is feeling the loss.

- Remain positive with your son and allow him to hear your words of confidence and trust in his heavenly Father. It will be important that he see you leaning on God as the ultimate protector, comforter, and provider.

- Focus on what he *does* have. For starters he has a caring, loving mother.

- Do not try to make up for the void of a missing father by granting his every whim and desire. Never make decisions out of guilt, or you will trade one problem for a bigger one. If you try to compensate for the loss of his father by spoiling him or buying him whatever he wants, your actions will imply that loose rules or material possessions will fill the void.

- If you are dating, do not introduce new men to him with great expectations that they will fill the void in your son's life. Be careful about the timing of involving men you are dating in your son's life, as it will create more pain and instability should the relationship not work out.

If Your Son's Father Is Present in the Home But Absent

I realize that some mothers reading this book are in a similar situation as single mothers in that their sons' biological fathers are living in the home, but they are absent for all practical purposes when it comes to rearing their sons. I want to be sensitive to the fact that many wonderful, caring mothers do not have a husband who is fully engaged in the parenting process. Many mothers carry the burden of training their sons in spiritual matters alone. It is especially tricky when it comes to training your son in matters where Dad's example conflicts with God's teaching. If you are such a mother, you have my respect and admiration. Here are some things for you to consider:

- Be careful not to bad-mouth your husband's lack of involvement in spiritual matters. In the end, you want your son to remember most your godly example and devotion to training him spiritually rather than your bitter words regarding his father.
- Refrain from badgering your husband to spend more time with your son(s). Never compare your husband to other fathers to provoke him into action. Take your frustrations straight to God and ask God to change your husband's heart. There is nothing wrong with making a gentle and godly appeal to your husband, but repetitive suggestions to guilt him into action will not be fruitful in the end.
- As you encounter situations where you and your husband do not hold the same spiritual convictions, ask for your husband's blessing and support as you try to raise your son to be godly.
- Make your church's youth minister aware of your husband's lack of involvement in your son's spiritual training. Ask your youth minister to expose your son to

positive male role models when possible. It is critical that your son witness godly male role models who can give him a visual of what it means to be a godly man.

- Trust that your son will be intuitive when it comes to recognizing his father's spiritual emptiness as the years progress. Again, make an effort to emphasize your husband's good qualities so as not to drive a permanent wedge between father and son.

Whether your son's father is absent altogether or present in the home but absent when it comes to spiritual training, the most important thing you can do to make up for the lack of a positive father role model is to expose him when possible to other godly male role models. As he encounters godly Sunday school teachers, scout leaders, coaches, neighbors, and the like, point out their positive qualities so your son can get a visual representation of what it is to be a godly man. Pray faithfully that as your son grows, he will reflect on the examples of the godly men he witnessed along the way and seek to implement the positive examples in his life.

Most importantly, whether or not you have the luxury of a husband who accepts God's role for him as a father, pray that Malachi 4:6 will be fulfilled and that God will turn the hearts of fathers to their children. Our sons will thrive best when they have fathers who are godly role models, but should they not have this benefit, it is not a lost cause. Boys are highly influenced by their mothers and fiercely loyal to them. Never underestimate your calling and impact as a mother in the effort to raise your son to be godly.

CHAPTER 3

A Mother's Sphere of Influence

It is my conviction that many a mother will
occupy a higher position in God's kingdom than
many prominent Christian leaders whom we might
expect to find in places of greater honor.
Think of some of the great men of the Bible like Moses,
Samuel, and Timothy. Where would they have been had it not
been for their praying, Spirit-led mothers? Think of Augustine,
John Newton, and the zealous Wesleys; their names may
never have lighted the pages of history had it not been for
the blessed influence of godly mothers!
The simple prayers from our infant lips were but echoes
from our mother's heart. Can we ever forget the soft caresses
of those hands of blessing on our heads as we knelt by our beds?
Can we fail to remember her night vigils, her seasons of intercession,
her well-marked Bible, and her words of admonition? Her actions
spoke eloquently of Him who taught us of the greater love of God.
What a tragedy to neglect the counsel of a godly mother!
What eternal consequences to reject her God! "Do not forsake
the law of your mother" (Prov. 1:8).

—HENRY G. BOSCH[1]

I find it interesting that in 2 Kings, when the reign of a new king was introduced, the name of his mother was often included. With each king we are told that he either "did what was good in the eyes of the Lord" or "did what was evil in the eyes of the Lord." Can you imagine if we were to look over our respective family trees and find listed beside the name of each deceased relative one of the two phrases, "did what was good in the eyes of the Lord" or "did what was evil in the eyes of the Lord"? Further, what if we were to find the mother's name of each relative listed directly beside the phrase?

I am certainly not suggesting that mothers are to blame if their children choose not to do good in the eyes of the Lord. I have known plenty of godly mothers who were devoted to the spiritual training of their children only to have the heartbreak of one or more of their children becoming prodigals. Our children will ultimately make their own decisions regarding matters of faith.

In this chapter we will examine the tremendous calling God has placed on our lives as mothers to impact our sons to be the godly men of the next generation. Moms have an opportunity to influence their sons in ways a father cannot. But to raise our sons to be the godly men of the next generation, we must devote ourselves to this high calling with purpose and determination, under the direction and power of the Holy Spirit.

Mom, the Emotional Facilitator

An ancient proverb says, "A mother understands what a child does not say."

On a recent afternoon my younger son, Hayden (sixth grade), climbed into my car after school and announced, "I just had the worst day ever." He went on to share the long list of grievances that contributed to his worst-day-ever state of mind. He started with, "Some girls in my grade said I'm mean," which led him to believe, "No one likes me." He made a heart-wrench-ing statement that "at basketball practice, some of the fifth graders on my team called me a shrimp." When he was finished, I did what any decent mother would do: empathize with him by offering soothing and compassionate words. I bit my tongue and refrained from offering a practical and relevant "sixth-grade girls are psycho" and "the younger boys on your team are just jealous." I commended him for sharing his feelings and told him something that I had picked up at a parenting course held at my church years ago: "Everyone will experience hurts, but the saddest thing is to hurt alone."[2] My poor oldest child didn't get the benefit of such wisdom on my part and was subjected to never-ending pep talks (lectures) laden with Bible verses. It's a wonder he will come to me at all today!

Like it or not, Mom is usually the emotional facilitator of the home. Our job duties include everything from bandaging our kids' boo-boos, mediating their quarrels, mending their broken hearts, and cracking the cryptic code of the emotions behind their silence. Our response will set the tone for how our kids will respond to emotional situations. And as if that is not pressure enough on us, our kids will more than likely follow our example in their own marriage and parenting.

Here are some sure-fire ways to send your boy the message that his feelings and emotions are not welcome in your home.

When your son shares a hurt:

- Respond with facts, logic, and reason.
- Ask him what part he played to bring about the hurt.
- Quote numerous Scripture verses to him and cliché him to death with "What would Jesus do?"
- Minimize his hurt with comments like "Don't be so sensitive" or "Don't take it so personally."
- Shame him with platitudes like "Big boys don't cry," "Buck up little camper," or "Be a man!"
- Attempt to take his mind off of matters by giving him something or distracting him with an activity. ("Why don't you go play X-Box to take your mind off of it.")

With that said, distraction is not a bad idea once you have addressed the problem and comforted his hurt.

- Act as if he is a burden with comments like "I don't have time for this!"
- Breach his trust and share his hurt with others.

I am sure we have all been guilty of responding to our sons' hurts in one or more of the ways above. Before taking the parenting course at my church, I was guilty of responding to my sons' hurts with many of the ways above. When I stopped to consider how I would want someone to respond to me when I share a hurt (spoken words of comfort and compassion), it made sense that others would prefer the same response. Yet my tendency when my sons shared their hurts was to attempt to fix the problem and make it all better. By habit, I still catch myself from time to time launching into a quick-fix solution when one of my sons shares a hurt. Recently, Hayden called me to the carpet and said, "Mom, I don't really want you to tell me what to do right now. . . . I just want to be angry." Wow, I've certainly felt that way before.

If, upon reading this, you have determined that you are in the habit of responding in an improper manner to your son's hurts, it is not too late to change. I certainly don't want to oversimplify the solution to addressing hurts, but once you get the speech down and work hard to replace unhealthy responses to your son's hurts with healthy responses, before long it becomes habit.

Start by being open and honest with your son and humbly share that you have not always responded appropriately to his hurts in the past. Further, ask him to be patient with you as you work on this area of your life. Give him permission to tell you, "Mom, I really just want you to say you're sorry that I'm feeling sad rather than give a bunch of advice."

Now, this is not to say that advice does not have its place. After you have appropriately empathized with your son ("Son, I am so sorry you had a bad day. Why don't you tell me about it?"), giving some brief counsel is appropriate. He is more apt to receive it if he feels his hurt has been acknowledged and validated. ("Son, I can certainly see why you would feel sad over that. I would feel sad too.")

When you reply to your son's hurts with empathy and validate his feelings, it's amazing how it becomes a welcome mat for him to share future hurts. He realizes that you are a safe person when it comes to processing his fluctuating emotions and feelings. On the other hand, if you continue to respond to your son's hurts in ways that minimize his feelings, it is only a matter of time before he will quit coming to you altogether. He would rather stuff his feelings and hurts than risk the even worse feeling of sharing his feelings and receiving an improper response.

Once I had empathized with Hayden about his "worst day ever," he was open to my suggestions as to how to address the issue. I shared with him that the middle school years are often the most difficult years of a child's life. I even used an example from my own life and told him, "You know, Hayden, you and I are a lot alike. Sometimes, when I get my feelings hurt, I imagine that things are much worse than they are. The truth is, some of the girls may think you're mean, but that doesn't mean that no one in your grade likes you." To support my point, I went on to name his good friends. By the time we pulled into the driveway, I had comforted his hurts, shared truth, and prayed with him. I topped it off with a big hug and even let him shoot some hoops before he started his homework. He was a different child from the one I had picked up that afternoon.

Later in the day I heard him actually tell a church friend about his day and say, "My mom says it's just a stage kids go through in middle school." Amazing. Now if I can just get him to keep bringing his emotional hurts to me through the difficult teen years!

You've probably heard the saying, "If Mama ain't happy, ain't nobody happy." How true it is! Mothers who have not learned to express their own emotions in a healthy manner will likely raise sons who do the same. If you have not learned to express your emotions properly, it's time to learn. I am living proof that it is never too late to do so. As someone who learned early on in my childhood to "stuff my problems," I was ill-equipped to deal with my children's hurts and insecurities. How thankful I am that God led me to sign up for the parenting course at my church. I shudder to think of the negative consequences my sons would have experienced had I not recognized that I had a problem and sought to correct it. I can assure you that I would not be experiencing the close communication I have with my sons today. My sons know that they can bring their hurts, insecurities, and problems to me (or their father) and their feelings will be acknowledged and addressed. As a result, they will never have to hurt alone.

Several nights ago Hayden and I went to Starbucks on a date of sorts. I wanted to catch up with him and see how things were progressing at school since his "worst day ever" had occurred. While we sipped on our vanilla latte and white chocolate mocha, he told me that things were much better at school. He even opened up some more with sentences like, "You know what really bugs me . . ." and "One thing I don't get about girls is . . ." On our way home I told him how proud I was that he would open up and share his feelings. I reminded him that his father and I are always available for him. When Hayden and I pulled in the driveway, he said, "Thanks, Mom. I hope I still want to hang out and talk with you when I'm older." I smiled as he got out of the car and quickly swiped a stray tear away before he noticed. "Me too, Hayden. Me too."

Mom, the Model of Womanhood

Andrew Jackson wrote of his mother:

> There never was a woman like her. She was gentle as a dove and brave as a lioness. . . . The memory of my mother and her teachings were, after all, the only capital I had to start life with, and on that capital I have made my way.

I find it daunting that a boy's introduction to the female gender will begin with *his mother.* Whether you like the thought or not, you will become the definition of womanhood for your son. You will leave an impression on your son, be it good or bad, that will play a part in molding his preferences for his future wife. Girls may think more about marriage and having children than boys, but rest assured, your son will ponder these things when the time draws near. He will take a mental inventory of his childhood and the part you played and use it to frame his desires for the future. If he remembers a mother who is warm and loving and who provided a home that was filled with laughter and happy memories, he will not be able to settle for less. He will have tasted the best that life has to offer and will seek it out for himself.

If, on the other hand, your son experiences a mother who is harsh, unloving at times, and too busy with her own life, he will not have a positive frame of reference. He may sense that there is something better than the impression he has been given but lack tangible benchmarks with which to measure the qualities and weaknesses of others.

We also must accept that our sons are unique individuals and may not choose to marry someone like us, even if we have done a bang-up job. Our job is to leave them with a positive impression of what it is to be a woman. Do you rejoice in being a woman? Do your children sense that you feel blessed and honored to carry the title of wife and mother? Or do they sense that you are burdened by these roles? Your son needs to witness a mother who loves, honors, and respects his father in order that he may have a picture of an intimate and caring marriage. He also needs to witness a mother who nurtures and cares for her children and relishes her title as mother. Even if you are a single mother, your child still needs to hear you speak positively of the institution of marriage as created by God.

Most important, our sons need to witness a mother who is at peace with herself and her God. Our warm smile, gentle touch, compassionate words, deep faith, and feminine ways will define womanhood to our sons. I rejoice in the blessing of being a wife and a mother, and pray that both of my sons will marry a woman who also esteems these roles. I realize that my attitude and example will play a huge part in molding their expectations for the future.

Mom, the Values Virtuoso

George Washington, the father of our country, wrote:

> I attribute all my success in life to the moral, intellectual, and physical education which I received from my mother.

In a 2002 nationwide survey of more than one thousand adults that was conducted by George Barna (the renowned pollster), a question was asked regarding the collapse of Enron, WorldCom, and other companies. Survey participants were asked what, in their opinion, would have helped avoid those collapses completely, mostly, only a little, or not at all. They were given six choices from which to choose. A large majority (72 percent) of the survey participants polled agreed that the problems could have been "completely" or "mostly" avoided had "parents spent more time teaching their children appropriate values." This topped such choices as: "business executives had better training in ethics," "government regulations were more demanding," and "American society had a stronger moral foundation."[3] The poll reveals that even the public-at-large recognizes the powerful influence parents can have in shaping the value systems of their children—value systems that will be carried into their families, workplaces, and communities.

Parenting a child has always been a challenging task but, arguably, never more difficult than today. Our grandparents, and, for the most part, our parents, had the privilege of raising their children in a culture that was generally based on the Christian value system upon which our nation was founded. Today we find ourselves swimming upstream in a culture that is tolerant of all value systems but the Christian value system. For the most part, God has been removed from the workplace, public schools, and government.

How could this have happened when, even today, surveys show that approximately 84 percent of Americans claim to believe that Jesus Christ is God or the Son of God and 61 percent say, "Religion can solve all or most of today's problems"?[4] Why are Christians so strangely silent? As mothers (and Christians), we must be willing to speak up and say, "Enough!" We must recognize the responsibility and power we have been given as mothers to shape an entire generation.

George Barna recently said:

> More than many people want to admit, how we train our children determines their values, views and behaviors as adults. If you want a moral society, you must develop it by raising children who understand and embrace good values and standards.[5]

It is not enough simply to determine that we will raise our sons to be moral and upright. We must set forth with a purpose and plan that properly defines "good values and standards."

Mom, the Most Revered Figure in Her Son's Life

Henry Wadsworth Longfellow wrote:

Even He that died for us upon the cross, in the last hour, in the unutterable agony of death, was mindful of His mother, as if to teach us that this holy love should be our last worldly thought—the last point of earth from which the soul should take its flight for heaven.

Many studies reveal that the most formative years of a child's life are the earliest years. It is clear that mothers have a tremendous influence on their children when they are young. What child doesn't adore his/her mother when he/she is young? When my son Ryan was a toddler, he would tell me, "Mom, when I grow up, I'm going to marry you." Now in high school, this same child instructs me to walk ten paces behind him in public lest anyone see him out with his *mother* and mistake him for a mama's boy.

But here's a news flash to mothers who wonder if the prime years of influence end with the onset of the teen years: George Barna, in his book *Real Teens*, says, "Although millions of mothers of teens would faint at the idea, Mom is typically the most revered figure in the life of a teenager."[6] Get out the smelling salts. This mother is shocked but encouraged. Further, when Barna surveyed teens and asked what grade they would give their moms for their parenting prowess, 75 percent gave their moms an A, 20 percent awarded their moms a B, and just 6 percent gave their mothers a C or lower.[7] Clearly, they are watching, listening (even past the statement "Mom, give me a break"), and looking for direction.

In Deuteronomy 6:4–9, Moses exhorted the Israelites with the following challenge concerning their responsibility as parents:

Hear, O Israel: The LORD our God, the LORD is one. Love the LORD your God with all your heart and with all your soul and with all your strength. These commandments that I give you today are to be upon your hearts. Impress them on your children. Talk about them when you sit at home and when you walk along the road, when you lie down and when you get up. Tie them as symbols on your hands and bind them on your foreheads. Write them on the doorframes of your houses and on your gates.

God expects the same of Christian moms today. He is much more concerned that our sons receive proper training in his truths and principles than a coveted spot on the A team, their name on the honor roll, or even a college degree. While these things are worthy, they should not be our primary focus.

Given the times, it is more important than ever that Christian moms are purposeful about the spiritual training of their sons. It is not enough to take them to church, put them in Christian schools, and/or say bedtime prayers. As mothers appointed by God to raise his boys in today's world, we must set forth with purpose and determination. We must have a clear understanding of God's truths in order to impress them on the hearts of our children. Impressing God's truths on our children involves teaching them with our words and showing them with our actions. In other words, we must practice what we preach and preach what we practice.

According to a Purdue University study that examined how parents influenced the religious beliefs of students eighteen to twenty-five, it is not enough for parents to model their beliefs to their children if they want them to adopt their religious beliefs. "Parents have to talk about those beliefs and share their thoughts with their child," according to Lynn Okagaki, who conducted the study. The study revealed that children were more likely to adopt their parents' beliefs when they had a clear understanding of what their parents believed.

If we are to counteract the negative influences of the culture, we must be armed with God's truths and teach them to our sons. We must talk about God's truths when we "sit at home and when [we] walk along the road, when [we] lie down and when [we] get up." And we must do so in the hearing of our sons. A mother who passes down God's truths to her children can literally have an impact on the souls of future grandchildren and great-grandchildren for generations to come. God has equipped us with everything we need to accomplish his purposes in our sons' lives. If we rely on the one perfect parent for guidance and strength, we will be able to parent our sons effectively. Hide that truth in your heart as we focus in part 2 on specific challenges our sons face in today's culture.

HOT WHEELS TO HORMONES . . . AND BEYOND

CHAPTER 4

Moms Who Cleave Raise Boys Who Can't Leave!

When my younger son, Hayden, was eighteen months old, he was accidentally left behind on a soccer field. At the end of my older son's game, I left with my daughter to take my car in for repairs. The plan was for my husband and the boys to meet us at the dealership.

When my husband arrived at the dealership and walked in with my older son, Ryan, my maternal instincts immediately kicked in. He was not the type to leave a sleeping baby in a parked car, but I assumed this could be the only reason for my son's absence. When I asked my husband, "Is the baby asleep?" I immediately knew the answer by the look of sheer panic on his face. Before he could even finish saying, "I thought you had him!" I was out the door with my daughter and heading at high speed to the soccer field five miles away.

A thousand thoughts went through my mind in that seemingly never-ending trip to field. The field was bordered by a fence, and on the other side was a busy road. Did he attempt to follow his father outside the fenced area where the car was parked? What would I find when I arrived? Ambulances with sirens blaring? I wept and prayed aloud, pleading with God for his safety. My poor daughter was only four at the time and witnessed a different side of her mother. In the mix of hysteria, one thought shadowed all the others: my baby was alone and, as his mother, I had to get to him.

In a matter of minutes, I had pulled up along the side of the soccer field just in time to see my husband running across the field to a woman who held our baby in her arms. (To this day I have no clue how he could have beaten me to that soccer field.) I watched from my car as the woman handed my baby over to my husband. At that moment I literally collapsed. I was unable to move from my car, and my husband ended up leaving his car at the field and driving our family home. I sat in the back seat next to Hayden in his car seat as he quietly sipped apple juice from his Tommee Tippee cup, unaware of the magnitude of the moment. When we arrived home, I tucked my baby in his bed for a nap and went to bed myself. I was physically and emotionally spent.

In the days that followed, I would be moved to tears at the mere thought of what could have happened. I would awaken in the middle of the night with nightmares where I was separated from my son and unable to find him. In order to get back to sleep, I would go into his room and watch him while he slept, thanking God for a happy ending. A decade has passed, yet it is still uncomfortable to relay the story. I experienced firsthand the innate sense that God gives mothers to protect and nurture their children and the trauma that results should that bond be interrupted.

As mothers, our nature is to cleave to our children, especially in the younger years. As they get older, we must begin the painful process of slowly weaning them from our constant care in order to equip them for their eventual flight from the nest. At the same time our children begin slowly to pull away from us as they gain their independence and try their wings while under our watchful protection. There is little to prepare a mother for this painful and confusing transition. While our nature tells us to cling tight, in our hearts we know we must let go. We do our children a great disservice if we fail to do so.

I realize that those reading this book will have sons of varying ages. Some of you have young boys who still cleave to you, and it is hard to imagine a day when they will begin to pull away. Others have sons who are taking some sample flights from the nest, and you know firsthand this confusing season of life. I am currently in this season of life with my older son, and while I celebrate his milestones of independence, I also grieve his waning need of my care. Daily I must resist the temptation to hover over him, especially when he exits the house with car keys in hand.

Mothers who cleave to their boys will raise boys who struggle to leave, physically and emotionally. There are many ways mothers cleave to their sons. Below you will find profiles of cleaving mothers. Do you match any of the profiles? If so, the first step is to acknowledge that your cleaving is out of balance. Without doing so, it will be impossible to improve. You may even consider allowing your husband to read over the descriptions and give you an honest appraisal. The truth may hurt, but it's better to know now and take action than to watch your son suffer the consequences when he leaves the nest.

Little League Mom

You've seen her in action. Maybe you've even been her. She's every coach's nightmare, especially if, heaven forbid, the coach fails to notice her son's athletic abilities. She's the mom who fights her son's battles, many of which she starts herself. She believes in her son and wants what's best for him. Nothing wrong with that, but it gets out of hand when she bullies, manipulates, or even sweetly cajoles others to give her son preference over the others.

Just as James and John's mother had the nerve to ask Jesus if he would give her sons preference by allowing one to sit at his right and the other at his left in the kingdom, we too have been guilty of making unreasonable requests. Whether it is academic, athletic, or recreational, we want our boys to be treated fairly.

We will not serve our sons' best interests in the end by taking up their every battle.

If there is ever a lesson I have learned the hard way, it is that life is not always fair when it comes to my children. I have spent days seething over the unfairness exhibited toward my boys on the football field, the basketball court, and the baseball field. Whether they sat on the bench, batted late in the lineup, or were placed in positions that did not take advantage of their obvious skills, it was guaranteed to elevate my blood pressure and leave me grumbling in the stands. I have since improved my attitude and relegated myself to the cold, hard fact that sometimes things don't make sense. As I reflect with a newfound objectivity on some of the past battles I fought on behalf of my boys, I realize that in some cases I had imagined their skills to be far better than they actually were. In other cases it boiled down to a jealousy that my boys were not treated as well as some of their peers. In the end, I highly doubt my interference altered their lives.

A friend of my husband's is the commissioner of the local Little League organization. He commented once that the most difficult part of his job was dealing with the mothers! I realize there are valid cases where a coach/instructor/teacher is unfair, unreasonable, or just plain inept, and at times it may be appropriate to intervene on behalf of your son's best interests, but such times should be few and far between. If your son constantly hears you questioning or bad-mouthing the coach's/instructor's/teacher's strategies or decisions, he may falsely assume you will be there to fight his battles. Should there be a legitimate concern, it is far better to train our sons to speak up in a respectful manner to whomever is in charge. Whether our boys fail to make the A team when they clearly deserved it, sit on the bench for most of the season, receive a failing grade for school work, or are overlooked for a part in the upcoming school play, it can be a valuable opportunity to train them to handle uncomfortable situations and equip them for inevitable heartaches in the future. A day may come when he is unfairly passed over for a deserved promotion, gypped out of his apartment deposit, or something else equally unfair, and "Little League Mom" will not be there to pick up the pieces.

Many boys view it as the ultimate embarrassment to have their moms intervene even for noble purposes. Some may even grow to resent their mothers for doing so. My days of ranting and raving from the stands came to a screeching halt at a basketball game for Ryan many years ago. The official made one unfair call after another and, along with many other parents, I let my opinions be heard, even at one point yelling, "Oh c'mon! Is your nephew on the other team?!"

After the game a mother from the other team walked up to me with a smile and said, "Are you Vicki Courtney?" Against my better judgment I said yes, and she proceeded to tell me that her church was doing my *Virtuous Woman* Bible study. Key word: *virtuous*. She went on to say how much she was enjoying the study and sincerely thanked me for writing it. To this day I have no idea if she witnessed my anything-but-virtuous behavior, but I have no doubts that God used her to convict my heart. Today I am a new person at my son's sporting events. When the temptation comes to sound off to a coach or official, I retreat to my car and breathe into a brown paper sack.

Lifeguard Mom

I remember some years ago when a mom chewed out a neighbor who had banished her teenage sons from his property after her boys took his paddleboat for a joy ride out on the pond behind his house. When the owner of the paddleboat knocked on her door and reported the stunt, he was met with crass obscenities and the age-old "boys will be boys" excuse. This "Lifeguard Mom" threw out the swim ring and not only rescued her boys from the consequences of their wrongdoing but also excused their bad behavior! Is it any wonder that in the years that followed, these boys lived up to their "punk kid" reputations? The police visited their home on several occasions, and it was clear that the boys were under the assumption that someone (good ol' Mom?) would bail them out, literally. Unfortunately, their mother did them a huge disservice by rescuing them from necessary consequences.

When Ryan was a sophomore in high school, I received a shocking phone call one morning from the attendance office at his school. They were calling to confirm that I had written a note for Ryan to be released from school at noon for a dentist appointment. Most of Ryan's friends were in the B lunch period, and he had mentioned on several occasions that he would like to be in B lunch with his friends.

For a brief moment I considered owning the note and punishing him when he got home. Ryan had just been accepted as a candidate to the International Baccalaureate program, a rigorous academic track for honors students. I worried that a blemish on his record might affect his eligibility and thus have an impact on his college career. His stunt was especially unbelievable as he was an officer in the Fellowship of Christian Athletes.

The temptation to cover for him passed, and I told the attendance lady that I did not write the note. I grabbed my keys and headed to the school to see the note firsthand. I resisted the temptation to send him the following text message: "u r busted. grounded 4 life."

As luck would have it, I just happened to enter the attendance office to find Ryan, with his back to me, digging through a stack of excused hall passes, one of which he was hoping would be his. Not finding it, he then asked the attendance lady why his pass was not in the stack.

Still out of his sight, I patiently watched the drama unfold. She asked for his name, and when he told her, she said, "Oh, yes—Ryan Courtney. We called your mom because your note looked suspicious, and she's on her way up to the school."

Hearing my cue, I chimed in, "That would be me." Ryan slowly turned at the sound of my voice, the color completely drained from his face. You could have heard a pin drop in the office as I walked up to the counter and said, "C'mon Ryan, let's go take a look at the note together."

Ryan followed me behind the counter as they handed me the note. I looked over the note and without hesitation said, "This note is a forgery. What is our next step?" We were directed to meet with the vice principal, who gave Ryan a stern lecture and a mandatory Saturday detention.

It was one of the toughest things I have ever had to do. Before Ryan returned to class, I reminded him, "There is nothing you could ever do to make me or Dad stop loving you." I also reminded him that God felt the same way and had provided forgiveness for his wrongful actions. I hugged him and told him that he should make things right with God. With a tear in his eye, he hugged me and told me that he was glad that he had been caught.

On the way home I thanked God for giving me the strength to stand firm and resist the temptation to be a "Lifeguard Mom" and throw my son a lifeline. In the end, Ryan's actions did not have an impact on his academic standing, but even if they had, I would have handled the situation the same way. We must never forget that our sons' character is of far greater importance than their academic standing. Ryan is clear that his dad and I will not bail him out of consequences that result from poor choices he might make.

Roller-Coaster Mom

I doubt that Isaac's wife, Rebekah, was ever nominated for "Mother of the Year." Who can forget her stunt to gain for her favored son, Jacob, the blessing of Isaac that was intended for her other son, Esau? Not only was Rebekah guilty of showing favoritism to one of her sons, but she manipulated her son in a plan to fool her husband. While her sincerest motivation may have been love for her son, Jacob, it showed a lack of respect for her husband and put Jacob in a position where he disrespected his father. Rebekah displayed an unhealthy attachment to Jacob and taught him the art of manipulation as a means to an improper end. Sure, Jacob got his father's blessing by agreeing to participate in his mother's plan, but he ended up fleeing from his brother's wrath as a refugee on the run. It's a wonder this mama's boy survived those initial days sleeping alone on the desert floor with a stone for a pillow. I'm sure his mother never imagined that her dishonest plot would produce such a tangled web and leave her without her beloved son for many years to come.

Some mothers show a similar form of manipulation when they lean on their sons to meet their own emotional needs. Boys will naturally adore their mothers, and mothers can sometimes take advantage of their sons' devotion as a substitute for their own unmet needs. This is especially common in situations where the husband is absent or fails to meet his wife's emotional needs. Regardless, it was never God's intent for a child to meet the emotional needs of a parent. Does this mean a mother should never cry in front of her son or should refrain from sharing disappointments? Absolutely not. The key is balance. To shield your son entirely from seeing you express emotion or disappointment may lead him falsely to assume that the expression of emotions is unnatural.

Mothers with wavering emotions should not drag their sons along on their emotional roller coasters. If you are reading this and fear that you may fit this profile, you should consider seeing a licensed professional Christian counselor who is qualified to help you with your wavering emotions. You owe it to yourself and your family. "Roller-coaster moms" should never force their children to ride with them.

Personal Assistant Mom

I recently began to wonder if my older son, Ryan, could make it on his own without me to stock the pantry, buy his clothes, make his haircut appointments, and assist him with various other life skills. The thought hit me as we began the college search and application process. In a panic that arrived better late than never, I began the tedious process of weaning my boy from his personal assistant, yours truly. My first clue that the weaning process was going to be a bit tougher than I first imagined came one day when he announced that he needed a haircut. Now I realize this alone may seem impressive, but let me assure you, I had been riding his back for at least two months prior to this announcement. His hair had transitioned from "moppy cute" to "beware: small creatures may be nesting here."

With this profound declaration that he needed a haircut came a new and unfamiliar response from his mother: "Here is the business card of the person who normally cuts your hair. Give him a call and schedule an appointment." The reaction that followed would make the average person wonder if I had told him to break down the atom and document his findings. He grumbled, he complained, and he begged me to do it for him. Mind you, the lad would know best when he could schedule a haircut as the designated master of his day-timer and, on top of that, he can drive. I gently reminded him of the above truths, and finally he broke down and made the call—after numerous questions like: What do I say when they answer? and What if he doesn't work on the days I can come in? I helped him script his answers, and he was ready to go. I did, however, cave in on the day of the appointment when he begged me to meet him there and explain to the stylist how he likes it cut. I know, I'm a softie. Next time I'm holding firm.

And get this, a couple of weeks later, I told my then-eleven-year-old son, Hayden, that it was time for a haircut; handed him the same business card, and told him to call the number and schedule an appointment. I gave him three possible days and times, and without hesitation he took the card and made the call! A few minutes later he reappeared and said, "Mom, the appointment is at 5:00 on Monday." Wow, and to think I could have weaned Ryan earlier!

From their youngest years we have cared for our boys' every need from wiping runny noses and tying loose shoelaces to late-night runs to the store for poster board for the school project due the next day. Before long it becomes a part of who we are. Sometimes we complain and wonder if a day will come when we can clock out, but deep down inside many of us are not ready for the alternative: *not* to be needed. As a result, we continue to play the part of "Personal Assistant Mom" long after our sons need one.

Like creatures of habit, we fail to stop and ask ourselves if what we are doing for them is something they actually can, and should, do for themselves. We just keep doing what we do best . . . doing and doing and doing. And while our service may seem noble, if we fail to wean them from their state of dependence they will be unable to stand on their own. I realize that this is easier said than done, and as I type this, I have a mental picture of Ryan away at college when he begins next year. The setting is a dorm room, and he is picking up items of clothing one at a time from a giant pile on the floor and sniffing them. He settles for the one that smells the least bad and leaves for class. Wrinkled and unkempt, he runs his hands through his moppy hair on his way out the door. It is below freezing, and he is wearing his signature flip-flops. He owns tennis shoes, but they no longer fit due to the fact that his mother is not there to remind him to clip his toenails. God love him.

Holy Spirit Mom

One of the most difficult areas for me when it comes to letting go is when it comes to my sons' spiritual development. My prayer for my boys has always been that they will not ride Mom and Dad's spiritual coattails and will come to a place where they choose to make Jesus Christ the Lord of their lives. My husband and I have been diligent in training them by word and example consistently to pray, read their Bibles, attend church, tithe, and so forth. In addition, my husband disciples our boys separately (I have also discipled my daughter). I do not share that in any way to pat ourselves on the back but rather to make the point that in spite of our proactive parenting in spiritual matters, our boys are not unlike the average Christian boy who forgets his Bible nine times out of ten when heading out the door for church, sometimes cuts up in church, and would go days and possibly weeks without opening his Bible were he not reminded to do so.

It was so much easier when our boys were younger and I could choose their music, their videos, and even get them to sit on my lap and listen to a good Bible story. You remember—the age where they do things that prove they are well beyond their years in spiritual maturity and give you the calm assurance that they will likely never stray from the path of God.

Ryan was such a child. I have countless videos of him "playing church" and preaching from the Bible as young as eight years old to a congregation of neighbor kids. He made his six-year-old sister sing a solo, but I did have to intervene when he told his three-year-old brother to pass an offering plate.

I was fully convinced that he would grow up and change his world for Christ. There would be no stopping this boy. What I failed to factor in was that someday he might not want to read his Bible or pray every day. He might want to listen to secular music. He might argue with me to see PG-13 movies. He might forget to invite his classmates to church. He might bring home friends who slip on occasion and say a bad word. Or, heaven forbid, he might even stray from the path of God and sin.

Gone are the days when I could control whether he read the Bible or prayed. I started off nagging him with constant reminders, "Read your Bible," "Invite so-and-so to church," "When was the last time you prayed?" With college around the corner, I must resist playing the part of "Holy Spirit Mom." Once there he will be responsible for setting his own alarm to get up and go to church, initiating his own time alone with God, and cultivating a consistent pattern of prayer. Will he do it? I pray he does, but if he doesn't, it will not be for lack of training and encouragement by his parents. Even though I won't be there to give him gentle nudges to read his Bible, pray, and make wise choices, I can still pray that God will nudge his heart and remind him on a daily basis of how much he is loved by God (and by us).

So how did *you* do when it comes to the profiles of cleaving moms? The truth is, most of us can probably identify with one or more of the profiles. Yet, if we are to raise our sons to be godly, we must slowly cease cleaving, let go, and encourage them to cleave to the one true God. To hang on would be to lay claim to something that does not belong to us. Regardless, nothing can prevent us from clinging tightly to our boys . . . within our hearts.

CHAPTER 5

It Was Easier When Girls Were Yuck

One afternoon while driving my younger son, Hayden (then in sixth grade), home from school, he caught me off guard with this question: "Mom, how old were you when you had your first kiss?" I hesitated to tell him, given the fact it had occurred at his same age. His question brought the memory back in an instant. I was with a group of friends at the movies and sitting next to Bobby Mallow, the sixth-grade popular boy and, rumor had it, a kissing bandit. He had recently asked me to "go steady" and rewarded my yes with his clunky silver ID bracelet, which I proudly wore on my wrist. I was busy chatting with my friend who sat on the other side when the lights in the theater dimmed. I was focused on the previews when, all of the sudden, Bobby reached over and grabbed my hand.

Thanks to my fifth-grade steady, Dorwin, I was no novice to this hand-holding stuff. On the second day of school, Dorwin had passed me a note that read, "I like you. Will you go with me? Circle yes or no." (You betcha, I still have the note!) He was a cute, scruffy boy who had proudly earned the title of "fastest boy in the grade." Sounded like good credentials to me, so I circled *yes* and passed the note back. Not unlike the unspoken rules of today's grammar school going-out romances, it officially meant that we would hardly say two words to each other from that moment forward. We would, however, hold hands under the lunch table, as agreed upon in one of the many notes we passed back and forth at the beginning of the year. The first time he grabbed my hand under that lunch table, I knew I was hooked. I think I had a perfect attendance record that year. In fact, I remember getting quite irritated at my mother for having the nerve to buy fold-over lunch baggies because they had been on sale. Didn't she know how important it was for me to be able to single-handedly shake a sandwich out of its bag?! For one month I had to rip my sandwich baggies open with my teeth. So much for trying to impress Dorwin!

Fast-forward a year later to the movie theater. I had been going through hand-holding withdrawals since breaking up with Dorwin some months prior, so it was nice to know it could still elicit the same jumpstart to my heart. As the movie wore on, I noticed Bobby beginning to scoot closer and closer until finally the sides of our heads were almost touching. Just as I was beginning to wonder what his motives were in leaning in so close, he let go of my hand and quickly put his arm around me. That was a new feeling. And a good one, at that. But before I had time to analyze this move, he turned toward me and with his other hand reached over and gently touched the back of my head, making it near impossible to escape the kiss that followed (as if I wanted to, anyway!). What ensued next was a tingle-down-to-your-toes, can't-catch-your-breath, movie star kiss. Fortunately, we both thought movie stars kissed with their mouths closed, so it stayed rather innocent.

When it was over, I was certain that my heart was beating loud enough for everyone in the theater to hear. I felt as if I was floating on air in some sort of half-awake, half-asleep state of mind. The kissing bandit had struck. That kiss minimized to a tiny spark the hand-holding jolt I had once felt. We broke up before there would be a second kiss, and I wouldn't kiss a boy again for at least another year. It didn't matter because I conveniently stored that kiss in my mind and would replay it from time to time.

As I was finishing that thought, I heard Hayden calling me back to reality. "Mom, mom, did you hear me? When was your first kiss?" I snapped out of my trance-like journey to the past and replied to Hayden, "Why are you asking? You are far too young to worry about such silly things!" *Wow, that should sway him from taking my same path*, I thought. I happened to know that he liked a girl who, rumor was, liked him in return. I also happened to know that they were both invited to a bonfire party that weekend. And with that thought, my mind raced back to a few bonfires I had attended . . . and hayrides . . . and school dances. Yikes! I had no choice but to head this off at the pass. "Hayden, I know you probably didn't know this, but kissing before marriage is outlawed in all fifty states. If you get caught, you could do serious jail time." Not buying it, he replied, "Ah, Mom. I just wanted to know how old you were—that's all."

Then it occurred to me what a blessing it was that he would even consider discussing the topic of a first kiss with me. And at that point I decided to take a risk. I told him the truth. "Hayden, do you *really* want to know how old I was when I had my first kiss?" He nodded his head, and I proceeded to tell him. I told him how it made me feel, and I confessed that my heart would still race days and even weeks later at the mere thought of that kiss. As much as I didn't want to tell him, I leveled with him and told him it was perfectly normal for a kid his age to be curious about kissing and maybe even want to kiss. More important, I told him that I was far too young for that kiss and the emotions that followed. I shared that the earlier you kiss, the more you dwell on the next kiss, and the next, and the next. I told him how, after awhile, it becomes less and less special and eventually you look for other ways to get that same thrill— things that should be saved for marriage. The lecture seemed to go over pretty well, and because I was honest about my own feelings at his age, he never really caught on that it was a lecture. Best of all, it opened the door for future conversations regarding girls.

If your son doesn't come to you with his girl issues, let me assure you that you are in good company. Hayden is a rarity, and much of his openness is due to his temperament. As the years wear on, I expect him to initiate fewer conversations, and I realize the importance of taking advantage of his open curiosity. In fact, I don't recall his older brother, Ryan, ever seeking my advice regarding girls. He gets my advice all the same, but I have to take advantage of teachable moments and initiate the conversations. Even so, sometimes he heeds my advice, and other times he insists on learning some things on his own. If he absorbs one-tenth of what I tell him, it is better than nothing. I am a firm believer that mothers owe it to their sons not only to model the beautiful qualities of womanhood but also to help them recognize these same qualities (or lack thereof) in other women. Then, when it comes time for their sons to choose brides, they will have had positive examples and much-needed counsel to aid them in their decisions. I also hope to have encouraged my sons along the way to become the kind of young men that all parents with daughters dream of having for future sons-in-law.

I am amazed at the number of Christian mothers who obsess over praying for their son's future wife but fail to recognize the duty they have in helping their sons develop healthy relationship patterns in the years leading up to marriage. It would be similar to praying diligently that your child will win a gold medal at the Olympics someday but failing to recognize the importance of consistent training in order to accomplish that goal. A gold medal is not likely if they have been left to figure things out on their own. With a divorce rate of nearly 50 percent, it's safe to say that few are getting the training needed on the front end to successfully navigate a marriage relationship. While children who have had parents who helped them develop healthy relationships are not exempt from the pain of failed marriages, they will be less likely to bail when the going gets tough. As mothers, we must leave our sons with the tools needed to understand the differences between guys and girls, make wise choices when it comes to the kinds of girls they date, behave nobly in dating relationships, and recognize positive qualities in their future mates. I will later elaborate on how to reach each of those goals. But first, let's go over some ground rules that must be in place. If practiced, it will create the kind of environment that lends itself to positive communication with our sons when it comes to matters of the heart. I call it the "never-ever list."

Never ever . . .

- Share anything he tells you with another mom or sibling.
- Tease him about liking a certain girl. You hated it when your parents did it, and he does, too.
- Push him to tell you more than he is comfortable sharing.
- Badger him to like a certain girl. It usually backfires anyway!
- Say/do things he would not want you to say/do in front of girls (this goes for pulling out the cute naked baby pictures or telling embarrassing stories!).
- Minimize the pain of a breakup. (Example: "It's probably for the best so you can focus on your studies more." "You have more important matters to worry about.") Such statements may be true, but ask yourself if what you are about to say to him would have offered you comfort at his same age after a painful breakup.
- Cease praying for your son.

From cooties to crushes and beyond, a mom can be a tremendous positive influence in her son's life, but first she must earn her son's respect by living an authentic witness to the truths she imparts to her son. Only then will she earn the right to be heard. Just as mothers in the Bible imparted advice to their sons regarding women, so should we. That having been said, I also realize that in many homes the dad plays the primary role in counseling his son regarding girl matters, especially when the son begins to pull away from the mom during the middle-school years.

One friend of mine shared that her son is more comfortable listening to dad, so she has stepped back. When she observes a situation that needs attention, she discusses it with her husband so he can address it with their son. In other homes (like mine), mom and dad both play a part in guiding their sons through girl matters. In yet other homes, mom is the primary influence, especially if it is a single-mom situation. Whether you influence your son from the front lines or behind the scenes is of little consequence as long as he is receiving positive and godly counsel.

Girls 101

I remember one of the first conversations I had with my son regarding the differences between guys and girls. He was going out with a girl at school and did not call her the entire Christmas break. He had cooled on the whole dating experience, especially when it became clear that he would have to use his own money to buy her a small Christmas gift. Rather than do the noble thing and give her the "let's just be friends" speech, he avoided her, somehow imagining the problem would go away before school started back up and he had to face her. My son had confided in me his desire to break up, and each day I would ask him if he had contacted her about breaking up. As the days wore on into weeks, I pointed out to him that this poor girl was likely checking her cell phone every few hours to see if he had called. She was not the type to call him, so she had no choice but to play the waiting game. Ryan minimized the whole deal, refusing to believe a girl would check her phone daily for a message or allow his vanishing act to cause her a moment's grief.

Finally, after several weeks of no contact, he called her and left a message for her to call him back. Almost immediately, she returned the call to his cell phone. At the time we were eating dinner, so we told him not to answer and call her back after dinner. When he finally listened to her message, his heart sank. She went on and on about how much she had missed talking to him over the holidays and mentioned that she had been checking her phone each day to see if he had called. (Can you hear me clearing my throat?) She ended her message with "I can't wait to talk to you!" Fortunately, he felt like pond scum, which is a huge indicator that he does have feelings. He honestly did not intend to hurt her but had innocently thought she would process things in a similar manner to a guy. He did what he could to minimize the damage, and they ended on good terms. Ryan learned a valuable lesson in the difference between guys and girls and the way they process things.

It came to my attention this past year that my younger son, Hayden, also has a long way to go when it comes to understanding the differences between guys and girls. He and a buddy of his decided to run for president and vice president of their sixth-grade class. As part of the exercise, they had to come up with a platform and present it in their campaign speech. The competition was stiff, and every vote would matter. As Hayden was busy preparing his speech one afternoon, I mentioned to him the importance of getting the female vote in order to win the election. At my prompting he and his friend put their heads together and came up with what they thought was a foolproof plan. "Mom, we are going to promise each girl a mechanical pencil if we are elected." Bless their hearts. I sat my son down and gave him a crash course on girls. (Translation: A mechanical pencil will not woo the average girl.) After giving it some more thought, they came up with the idea of promising each girl in their class a carnation and personally written poem, if elected. I don't even have to tell you the results!

On a more serious note, a few sixth-grade girls recently cornered my son and one of his friends and asked them who they thought was the prettiest girl out of the three of them. Each one insisted that she would not be mad or take it personally if she wasn't the one picked. Yeah, right. Fortunately, I walked in on this conversation just in the nick of time and put a cease to the folly. I explained to Hayden and his friend the dangers of participating in such silly games. Further, I assured them that the two girls not picked would forever remember it and probably end up lying on a black leather couch and reciting verbatim the content of that conversation to a therapist decades later.

I could share example after example of how I have had to coach my boys on how girls and guys perceive things differently. Whether it is a caution against teasing that goes too far, roughhousing, or comments that are perceived as hurtful, we must educate our boys to such realities. We cannot expect that they will somehow figure these things out on their own. God never intended that his girls be treated as "one of the guys." Our boys must be taught to respect these differences whether they understand them or not.

In addition, we need to warn them of common games many girls play (gossip, manipulation, jealousy, flirting, malicious behavior, etc.). Again, this is not to stereotype that all girls play such games, but the truth is, many do. I have warned my older son on many occasions to keep his eyes wide open when I suspect a girl is playing games with him. At the same time I have to be careful not to imply that all girls play games. I want my boys to appreciate the unique qualities God has given to women and enjoy the differences.

The Hanging-Out, Going-Out, Date-or-Not-Date Debate

Ask ten committed Christians their philosophy on dating, and you're likely to get ten different answers. I've lost track of the current trend among Christians. Should we encourage our teens to "kiss dating good-bye" or "give dating a chance"? There is, however, one thing that all ten of those Christians likely would agree on: Our culture's model of dating is not a healthy model for Christians. First of all, dating as we know it from our teen years is all but obsolete. Ask a sampling of high school or college girls how many official dates they have, and you're likely to find that few will need more than one hand to count them up. It's sad but true. So what are boys and girls doing if they aren't *dating*? Hooking up for one. Talk about a win/win for the guys. Girls pay their way; guys get their way, no strings attached. (We'll talk more about hooking up in chapter 8.)

Of course, as a woman, you know better. There are always emotional consequences for the girls. Whether a girl admits it or not, she wants to think she is important enough to merit a guy working up his nerve to ask her out, pick her up, pay her way, and hopefully, call her the next week. Girls were not wired for casual hookups.

Perhaps, the courtship (i.e., antidating) movement among Christians in the late 1990s was a response to the growing trend of hooking-up that was all too common. The antidating movement produced happy endings for some and disillusionment for others. At the time of the courtship wave, I was in ministry to college students, speaking to many groups across the country. I cannot tell you how many sharp, wonderful, Christian young men approached me with sad tales of how they had nobly attempted to ask their Christian sisters out on dates only to suffer harsh rejection. Some were even scolded for having the nerve even to think such a thing was possible. They would practically beg me to address the issue among the girls. On the one hand, courtship seemed extreme to me, but as a mother of soon-to-be teens at the time, I could certainly see its merits. However, as time wore on, the movement died down. It didn't prove to have staying power among the majority of Christian teens and singles. My guess is that it became clear to many that the odds of finding a suitor who embraced the same radical courtship ideals were highly unlikely. In Texas, we call this "slim pickin's." While a noble goal, girls who adhere strictly to courtship and the idea of waiting for a guy to jump through all the necessary hoops required by this model may find themselves waiting indefinitely. Likely, the only way courtship would work is if the environment in which the boy and girl are raised lends itself to such a model.

"Hanging out" now also appears to be popular among teens and is my personal favorite choice for my own sons. So important is this concept of hanging out in groups of friends to my husband and me that we added a game room onto our house when my son entered high school. When it was complete, we announced, "This is the hangout, and your friends are always welcome here." It has been a huge hit, not to mention a safe gathering place for my kids and their friends. While my son has had a few inconsequential girl relationships along the way, the majority of his high school years have been spent hanging out with his group of friends—both guys and girls.

While it is my preference that my own teenage kids hang out in groups, I am also not opposed to them "going out" on occasion. Several years ago I held the position that they would not be allowed to go out. As they got older, I realized that if handled properly with boundaries in place, the going-out experience can actually be a great training ground when it comes to future serious relationships.

Let me stress that this is what my husband and I have determined works best for our family. It may not be a good model in your home. In the end you will have to decide what is best for *your* child. Even so, I believe it is important to avoid being too extreme in your approach.

I had many lofty ideals on this subject when my children were younger. I even passed judgment on parents who allowed their teens to go out and silently branded them weak willed. Once my own kids reached an age where they expressed a desire to go out, God began to show me in my prayer time that my position on dating had more to do with my own fears that my children might make some of the same mistakes I had made in dating. Once I allowed God to minister to my fears, I began to reevaluate my position. I recognized that with the proper boundaries and training in place, going out could provide my teenagers with some experiences better learned and better dealt with while under my roof and supervision.

Again, this is the system my husband and I feel works best in our home. God may lead you and your husband to have an entirely different position based on your teenagers' unique temperaments and levels of maturity. The most important thing is that you come up with a system that both you and your husband agree upon and effectively communicate to your teenagers. Without a system in place, they will, by default, embrace the world's model of dating.

Is Kissing Evil?

One offshoot of the courtship movement was the "no kissing until marriage" philosophy. Though not wildly popular (no need to explain why!), it had some followers. While most mothers would be happy to see such a movement thrive, the reality is that few teenage couples will actually succeed in making it to the altar having never kissed. Again, this may work for some couples, but it is not right for everyone. In fact, I only know of a handful of couples that did not kiss until their wedding day, and two of the couples struggled with physical intimacy after marriage and had to see a counselor. We must be careful of extremes that imply there is only one way that pleases God and assumes that all others are sin. My advice to my own teenagers has been to save kissing for serious dating relationships.

Many Christian couples have remained sexually pure without giving up kissing. To do so, however, it is critical to have some rules in place to ensure that kissing does not lead down the slippery slope of sexual activity. Some good rules to consider are: avoid watching movies alone in dark rooms, do not sit in a car at night for long periods of time, do not lie down prone next to each other, and no snuggling under blankets. A mature Christian should be able to identify what conditions should be avoided. If your son is open to it, encourage him to have an accountability partner who will have the boldness to ask him some tough questions on a consistent basis.

Types of Dating to Avoid

Once you settle the dating debate and come up with a reasonable age to allow your son to date formally, you will need to help him define what constitutes a dating relationship that would honor God. It might help first to share types of dating relationships that don't honor God. Below you will find a slightly revised and adapted version of four types of dating that I cautioned young ladies to avoid in a Bible study I authored to college women, *Virtuous Reality: Becoming the Ideal Woman*. The same warnings hold true for our sons.

1. Dating for Fun—Guys should avoid dating someone simply for the sake of being able to say they are going out with someone. As mothers, we should teach our sons to understand that dating is something they should never enter into lightly. We should encourage them to focus on building friendships with girls, which is often best done outside the dating context and in group settings where they and the girls are free to be themselves.

2. Dating by Emotion or Physical Attraction—In high school, dating relationships usually begin based on nothing more than an initial physical attraction. Most guys enter into dating relationships based on physical chemistry more than facts or God's input. They rationalize that if it feels right, it must be right. Proverbs 4:23 provides a word of caution that our sons need to understand: "Above all else, guard your heart, for it is the wellspring of life." Part of guarding their hearts will be learning to trust God more than their emotions or hormones. God would not want our sons to become physically or emotionally intimate in a relationship that years later will most likely be nothing more than a faded memory with "ol' what's-her-name."

Hormones will often send a message that it feels right to pursue natural desires of the flesh or to give in sexually because of the erroneous belief that doing so will strengthen the relationship. Additionally, the culture readily preaches feelings as a litmus test for determining readiness to have sex. That alone should be a scary thought, given the fact that the average teenage boy, if he is honest, would probably say he feels like having sex. Mothers need to help their sons understand the dangers of entering into relationships based solely on emotion or physical attraction. They need to guide them to make godly decisions based on standards set forth in God's Word and the guidance of the Holy Spirit.

3. *"Joined-at-the-Hip" Dating*—Many dating relationships evolve into serious, long-term relationships that, in reality, emulate marriage. Often the couple will give up time previously spent with friends in order to spend more time together. This type of joined-at-the-hip relationship almost always leads to physical intimacy due to the amount of time spent together and the fact that the relationship seems like a marriage. I am amazed at Christian mothers who facilitate this sort of relationship by allowing their sons to spend too much time alone with their girlfriends. I realize that there are some dating relationships among spiritually mature teens that remain innocent and sexually pure, but they are the exception not the rule.

I have openly shared with my two older children of my own regret over having been involved in a serious "joined-at-the-hip" dating relationship in my high school years. We spent almost every waking moment together, swapped proclamations of love, and eventually gave up our virginity for each other. Even though I was not a Christian at the time, I knew in my heart that sex outside of marriage was wrong. Nevertheless, I mistakenly justified it because I thought we would someday marry and that somehow made it more acceptable in my heart and mind. Of course, like so many high school romances, the relationship ended within months of going our separate ways in college, and I haven't seen him since.

4. "Mission Field" Dating—Woe to the young man who compromises his Christian faith to date a young lady who is not a Christian! Second Corinthians 6:14 cautions against Christians being yoked together with unbelievers. While the Scripture is often used to support the conclusion that Christians should not marry non-Christians, it also applies to dating relationships. After all, most marriages are preceded by a dating relationship. If the "equally yoked" principle is followed in dating, it could spare our sons much heartache, especially if the relationship leads to marriage. I am amazed at how many Christian guys (and girls) ignore this verse because it would prohibit them from going out with someone they are physically or emotionally attracted to. Many guys innocently enter into dating relationships with non-Christians because they are unaware of 2 Corinthians 6:14, or because they believe it applies only to marriages. Mothers must be purposeful in sharing the concern about unequally yoked dating relationships *before* their sons begin dating. Our words of caution often ring hollow once they have fallen for someone who is not a Christian.

Be aware of one way Christian boys often justify dating non-Christian girls: They suggest they are dating the girls merely in an attempt to be a witness to and possibly lead them to faith in Jesus Christ. While it is possible for a Christian to lead a non-Christian to Christ in a dating relationship, this rarely occurs.

I witnessed a youth speaker illustrate this point by asking a student to stand on a chair. The student represented the "Christian" in the dating relationship. He then asked another student to come and stand on the ground next to the chair and for the two to clasp hands. The student on the ground represented the non-Christian in the dating relationship. The youth speaker asked the student on the chair to attempt to pull the other student up onto the chair while the other student was told to attempt to pull the "Christian" student down onto the ground. It doesn't take a rocket scientist to figure out how this experiment ended.

Am I suggesting that we should discourage our sons from befriending non-Christian girls and inviting them to Christian youth activities and church? Certainly not. But I am suggesting that our sons will be a more effective and consistent light for Christ if they are not entangled in relationships with non-Christian girls.

A Nice Guy's Dating Rules

Nice guys are not born; they are made. While dads will play a big role in modeling noble behavior to their sons, moms should never minimize the critical role they play. Don't wait until your son is about to enter into his first dating relationship and then give him a crash course in acceptable dating behavior. During my ministry to college women, I was disturbed at the number of young ladies who shared that "good Christian guys" are rare on their campuses and in their church groups. Many shared that the Christian guys were no different from the rest of the guys out there when it comes to rude behaviors, sexual joking, immaturity, and lack of respect for women. How sad. Christian parents must be purposeful in training their sons or, by default, their sons will follow the world's lead. Christians are called to be set apart from the world. That being said, moms (and dads) should consider passing down the "nice guy's dating code of behavior" to their sons and continue to hold them accountable to that code over the years. Some of these may seem out of date or old-fashioned, but if you have a daughter, I'm sure you'll agree that nothing less is acceptable for your girl!

Nice guys . . .

- Never ask a girl out via IM, text message, or e-mail.
- Never discuss details of the relationship with their friends, or anyone, for that matter. It will almost always come back to haunt them.
- Never flirt with someone else's girlfriend. There will be many insecure girls who initiate the flirting to bait the attention they crave, but most guys see through this behavior and recognize that they are one of many boys being flirted with.
- Stay true to their friends. If they are considering asking out a friend of a past girlfriend or a buddy's past girl-friend, they will wait a suitable amount of time and, if need be, give the friend or past girlfriend the heads-up beforehand.
- Will not engage in physical intimacies (hand-holding, kissing, etc.) with someone he is not going out with.
- Do not believe in "going Dutch" when they have a girl-friend. Some exceptions might be made (expensive concerts, etc.), but they should not be the rule.
- Make every effort to introduce themselves to the parents of the girl they are dating. With confidence and assurance, they know how to give a firm handshake to the girl's dad, make proper eye contact with him and the girl's mom, use proper manners ("Yes, sir," "No, ma'am"), be responsive to any questions they ask, and initiate conversation with them from time to time.
- Do not build a relationship with a girlfriend solely by means of IM and text messaging. Some conversations were meant to occur by phone call or face-to-face.

- Are not in the habit of belching, passing gas, swearing, and other abominable behaviors in front of the opposite sex. Girls should be treated as girls—not "one of the guys."
- Open car doors and doors, allow their girlfriends to pass through doors ahead of them, as well as display other common acts of courtesy.
- Never engage in sexual banter with the opposite sex. Insecure girls may laugh along with them, but deep inside they feel disrespected and devalued.
- Recognize the importance of prayer for making wise choices and avoiding temptations in a relationship.
- Flee tempting situations. No need to explain. If need be, they run for their lives and explain later.
- Never expect the girl they are dating to set the physical limits in the relationship. They have determined their own limits according to God, up front.
- Never end relationships over the telephone or by IM, e-mail, or text messaging. Further, they do not ask friends to deliver the bad news. If she was important enough to ask out in the first place, she is important enough to end the relationship in person.
- Behave nobly after the breakup. They do not vent their hurt or anger publicly or seek revenge.
- Treat past girlfriends with honor and respect. They do not betray them by sharing personal information with others.

There you have it. Are you raising a "nice guy"? If you see some signs in your son that cause you to believe the answer is no, it is not too late to try to teach him the ropes when it comes to relating to the opposite sex in a healthy manner.

Never underestimate the role you play in helping your son navigate these uncertain currents. The time you invest in helping him relate to girls will not return void. Even if he rolls his eyes, shrugs you off, or harasses you about the advice you give, persevere. There have been many times when I have imparted great motherly wisdom to my older son on matters involving girls only to be told, "Mom, you have no clue what you are talking about." Just recently he had the humility to admit that most everything I had told him had proved true or come to pass. With that he added with frustration and a smile, "It is so annoying!" And I thought he wasn't listening. He doesn't always follow my counsel, but clearly my words of wisdom were not forgotten.

CHAPTER 6

Searching for Worth in All the Wrong Places

Perhaps the greatest gift a mother can give her son is a proper foundation for establishing true worth. Unfortunately, many mothers are unable to give their sons something that they, themselves, do not possess. As a teenager, I was the type of girl who appeared to have it all. In the pursuit of self-worth, I jumped through every hoop the world held up. I was awarded such titles as cheerleader, class officer, and student council representative. My efforts earned me a coveted spot in the esteemed popular group and a steady boyfriend who drove a flashy Pontiac Firebird with t-tops (remember those?). As I grabbed each of these carrots that the world dangled before me in my endless quest for self-worth, it would satisfy for a time. Yet the boost in my self-worth was short-lived and never enough to satisfy fully. There was a vague awareness in my innermost being that something was missing.

Without an explanation of where true self-worth originates, by default I readily bought into the world's formulas. By the time I got to college, I had a conscious awareness of the futility that comes as a result of basing my self-worth on the world's formulas, but I was not aware of another alternative. Among other devastating consequences my self-paced quest for worth had left me with an eating disorder and had robbed me of my virginity. A major factor in my becoming a Christian at the age of twenty-one was the appeal that Christ would fill the empty places in my heart that resulted from the fallout of falsely defining my worth. I sensed that Jesus was much more than the answer to salvation that leads to eternal life. I sensed that he would provide the key to true self-worth. While my salvation was immediate, I did not experience true self-worth immediately. I grew impatient and frustrated that God's formula for self-worth did not provide overnight results. It was difficult to adjust my way of thinking to God's way of thinking after having been sufficiently brainwashed by the world's formulas since childhood. Like the proverbial dog that returns to its vomit, I ran back to the self-worth formulas that were familiar.

Some ten years after my salvation experience, I came face-to-face with the reality that I had continued even as a Christian to build my worth on a foundation of sinking sand. And the foundation was beginning to crack. My eating disorder once again reared its ugly head, and a general spirit of discontentment pervaded my life. Even though I had the knowledge that nothing but Christ could fully satisfy, my actions betrayed my knowledge of this truth. Unfortunately, I was not the lone victim. As a mother, I had unintentionally modeled to my children a willingness to trade God's truth for a lie. Oh, I could preach the truth in regard to where worth originates, but words mean little unless followed by actions.

> He feeds on ashes, a deluded heart misleads him; he cannot save himself, or say, "Is not this thing in my right hand a lie?" (Isa. 44:20)

At the writing of this book, it has been a decade since my rediscovery of the formula that leads to true self-worth. Though it has not been easy, with much effort and prayer I have finally come to base my worth on God's one true formula. There are times (how about turning forty?) when I slip back into my old ways and find myself not feeling pretty enough, smart enough, popular enough, or good enough. It is then that I stop and take a deep breath and remind myself of what Christ thinks about me.

Unfortunately, my children were influenced indirectly by my struggle with misdefined worth. Today I am making up for lost time by pointing out the fallacy of buying into the world's formulas for defining worth and passing down the only formula that matters—God's.

What is God's formula for defining one's worth? First, let's take a look at the world's formulas in order to gain a greater appreciation for God's one, true formula. You will quickly see that the quest for worth is not gender specific. Our sons are just as likely to base their worth on the world's formulas.

The World's Equations for Defining Self-Worth

1. Worth = What You Look Like. This formula is so pervasive in our culture, it is nearly impossible to escape. Boys may generally appear to feel better about their appearance than girls, but don't be fooled! Many experience the frustration that comes from measuring the culture's ideal with their own reflections in the mirror. I remember a time when my brother was in late grade school and I walked into his room and found him arm-hanging on the clothes bar in his closet just like he would on the monkey bars in the park. When I asked him what he was doing, he said he was trying to stretch his body to become taller! Just as girls may obsess over being too tall, too heavy, too flat-chested, our boys also struggle with their own checklist of insecurities.

One study of more than four hundred girls and three hundred boys in grades seven through ten found that body dissatisfaction is more common among females[1] and often results in a concern to lose weight.[2] Body image issues for males focus on gaining weight and shoulder/muscle mass.[3] Further, the desire among males to develop increased muscularity has emerged as an important issue among men and adolescent boys.[4] The study primarily focused on the direct correlation of three factors that resulted in body dissatisfaction. The three factors were media images, peer conversations, and peer criticism. Among boys, peer criticism was the greatest influencer in body dissatisfaction.

Before most boys enter high school, they will be clear on the culture's image of the ideal male. Tall, muscular, ripped abs, broad shoulders, and handsome facial features become the standard by which our boys will measure themselves. Some will appear not to care while others will hit the gym, insist on seeing a dermatologist, and pray for a growth spurt. I am convinced that inborn temperament explains why some boys are more dissatisfied than others. Both of my boys have been raised in the same home where both their father and I have diligently preached the mantra that worth should not be defined by outward appearance. My older son could afford to care a bit more about his appearance while my younger son needs to lighten up. I have, on occasion, chased Ryan through the house with a hairbrush and nail clippers only to be met with "Mom, I'm a guy!" His younger brother, on the other hand, has been flexing in front of his bathroom mirror since he was a toddler. At age twelve he does crunches at night to perfect his six-pack abs and would probably use a self-tanner if I would allow him to. (If only I could get him to care as much about brushing his teeth!)

I recently learned just how much Hayden is impacted by peer criticism. He shared with me that he liked a girl who supposedly liked him back. All was well until one of her friends passed on the news to Hayden that the girl had decided she couldn't like someone who is shorter than she is. My first instinct was to comfort him with the "you're not done growing yet" pep talk or tell him the story about an uncle who didn't have a growth spurt until college. Fortunately, before I opened my mouth, I realized that I was reinforcing the dysfunctional message that "worth = what you look like."

I chose instead to level with him. "Hayden, the truth is, you will probably be shorter than most of the guys in your grade." He has consistently tracked shorter than the average height on the charts at his yearly checkups, so why feed him with false promises that leave him feeling as if "shorter" is not adequate? I then asked him if he felt that God knew what he was doing when he created him. He nodded and mumbled a vague, "I guess." I went on to tell him that the truth is, most everyone has something about their appearance they would change if given the opportunity. "Hayden, there is nothing wrong with wanting to be taller, but if your worth becomes dependent on it, you will set yourself up for misery. The key is to see yourself through God's eyes, and God sees you as perfect." For extra credit I threw in, "And trust me, you are way too good for a girl who has such shallow standards."

Hayden is a lot like me. We both need encouragement from time to time when we slip back into the world's equations for worth. I found this to be true on a recent trip to the mall to get Hayden's hair cut. I was already gearing up for the familiar "worth doesn't equal what you look like" speech that is often necessary after a haircut.

We arrived early and had a half hour to kill before his appointment, so I decided to do some shopping. I ended up in the dreaded swimsuit department of a large department store. Yes, you guessed it, I somehow felt compelled to try on swimsuits! I know, I know, it would be less painful to run barefoot over shards of broken glass. Poor Hayden was left to wait outside the dressing room area, but he was not far enough away to escape my groans of displeasure as I tried on one swimsuit after another.

When I finally emerged empty-handed, he looked at me incredulously and said, "You tried on a bazillion swimsuits and didn't find one you liked?" Bless his little heart. If only it were so simple.

I responded with a quick, "The swimsuits were not the problem. As of this moment, I am officially on a diet." *Maybe, I thought to myself, I would even brush the dust off the elliptical trainer I purchased after swimsuit shopping last year and actually use it for its intended purpose.* Unused, it had conveniently become a clothesline for my hand-washables!

Without missing a beat, my sweet Hayden stopped, grabbed my wrist, and said, "Mom, worth doesn't equal what you look like, remember? You write about this stuff and teach it all over the country." Out of the mouths of babes. And for the record, two pairs of wet jeans are hanging on that elliptical trainer as I write this. So much for my bold proclamation!

As mothers, our first step will be an honest self-evaluation to determine if we have established a balanced perspective when it comes to the pursuit of outward beauty. Mothers who obsess over their weight, body shape, or appearance in general, and complain in the hearing of their children, send a message that supports the formula "worth = what you look like." God certainly never intended that we altogether ignore our appearance. There is nothing wrong with having our nails done, getting our hair highlighted, exercising to tone up, or slathering on the wrinkle cream before bedtime. In fact, we should seek to make the best of what God has given us and, in turn, teach our sons to do the same (like brush their hair and clip their toenails!).

When it comes to beauty, are we more focused on shedding the five pounds we gained over the holidays or having a regular daily quiet time of Bible study and prayer? Are we more focused on getting an extra hour of beauty sleep on Sunday morning or consistent church attendance? Are we more focused on making our nail appointment or our weekly Bible study? Most important, if we were to ask our sons whether our day-to-day actions indicate that we are more focused on what we look like on the inside or the outside, what would their answers be?

In *The Virtuous Woman*, I asked readers if they could stand in front of a full-length mirror while wearing their swimsuits and say, "I am fearfully and wonderfully made."

Our goal as mothers should be to raise our sons and daughters to say sincerely, "I praise you because I am fearfully and wonderfully made; your works are wonderful, I know that full well" (Ps. 139:14). Of course, they will be more likely to do this if we can claim the truth for ourselves. It's one thing to acknowledge that you are fearfully and wonderfully made but quite another to *know* it full well. Mothers who know it full well stand a greater chance of raising children who know it full well.

In addition, mothers would be wise to educate their sons early on to the sobering fact that kids will be cruel and will say things during their growing up years that are hurtful. While we cannot protect them from hurtful remarks, we can encourage them to choose their attitude when criticism comes (and it will). If we have been faithful to remind them that God has a different standard when it comes to measuring their worth, they will be better able to endure peer criticism that comes their way. Our sons need to be taught that being "fearfully and wonderfully made" is not conditional upon muscle mass, height, a clear complexion, or being labeled "hot" by the girls.

Our boys need to hear the story of the prophet Samuel, who was called by God to anoint a new king. He thought surely Jesse's handsome son Eliab was the Lord's anointed one. He had "future king" written all over him. Yet, in 1 Samuel 16:7, the Lord imparts these words of wisdom regarding outer beauty: "But the LORD said to Samuel, 'Do not consider his appearance or his height, for I have rejected him. The LORD does not look at the things man looks at. Man looks at the outward appearance, but the LORD looks at the heart.'" We should also allow our sons and daughters to hear us praise those who possess true inner beauty. While the world is quick to brand someone beautiful based solely on physical appearance, Christians should resist the urge and save the label for those who demonstrate true beauty that stems from the heart.

2. Worth = What You Do. I can vividly recall to this day the devastation I felt when I was not elected cheerleader in the seventh grade. I had readily bought into the world's formula that "worth = what you do," so I had determined that "cheerleader" was a label that guaranteed instant self-worth. By the time our sons reach middle school, they have learned what it will take to earn the world's applause. Are they talented, athletic, or smart? How many clubs do they belong to? Are they popular? Did they make the A team? When our sons base worth on what they do, accomplishments and titles become the necessary fix to ensure that they feel like they are something. While accomplishments can temporarily quench the desire for worth, the effectiveness wears off with each passing achievement. Surely, we all know people who in spite of countless achievements turn up empty in the end.

Unfortunately, most adults have bought into the world's formula that "worth = what you do," so they will naturally pass the dangerous lie on to their children. We have all witnessed parents who attempt to live vicariously through their children so they can selfishly say, "That's *my* kid." If you don't believe me, just head on out to the nearest Little League field. The same parents who are quick to take credit for their children's successes are also the ones who are chewing them up one side and down the other if they blow it. I joked with a counselor friend of mine that she ought to be handing her cards out to the grumbling parents in the bleachers at the local Little League field with a simple sales pitch of: "Hang on to this. Your child's going to need me someday."

Many parents rationalize that pushing their children to succeed will provide them with accomplishments that, in turn, will help them define their worth. I should know because I was the worst offender. When my daughter, Paige, was two years old, I signed us up for a mom and tot gymnastics class, hoping it would serve as an outlet to expend her boundless energy while at the same time give us an opportunity to spend time together. My dreams of mother-daughter bonding were dashed when on the first day of class she pushed me aside and said, "I do it myself." I was banished to the sidelines for the remainder of the class.

While other mothers and daughters were somersaulting down the mats, my little one kept wandering over to the three- and four-year-old class to do round-offs and handstands with the big girls. Within weeks the coaches gave in and put her in the older class, thus beginning her gymnastics career. She loved gymnastics, and it was clear from the beginning that she was a natural at the sport. At the age of five, she was invited to be on a show team that performs at local parades and events. The workouts were rigorous because they were grooming these girls for future competition. By the age of seven, she had been promoted to the highest-level performance team for her age group. I carted her off to gymnastics three times a week for classes totaling seven hours a week. Initially, Paige loved the costumes, performances, and applause, but within a few months of being promoted, she began to show signs of stress over the long workouts. Before long she began crying on the way to class. Rather than responding appropriately to her obvious cues, I instead gave her pep talks about the importance of persistence and hard work.

My moment of truth came one afternoon on the way to class, when through her tears she said, "I just want to be a kid and play with my friends after school." Ouch. As I pulled into the parking lot of the gym and saw her wiping away her tears in my rearview mirror, I came face-to-face with the cold, sobering reality that I was pushing her in gymnastics for all the wrong reasons. I wanted her to excel in something so that it would boost her esteem in the years to come. I rationalized that my own worth had benefited (albeit temporarily) from my success in gymnastics, and I wanted the same for her.

After many minutes had passed and many tears had been shed, I did the only thing I knew to do. I got out of my car, withdrew her from the class, and drove my daughter home. It was the beginning of a healing process—for both my daughter and myself. Once home, I apologized to my daughter for pushing her too hard and promised her that I was going to work on letting her "be a kid." The biggest test to my promise came just two weeks later, when she asked if she could join the gymnastics class her friends were in—a one-hour-a-week beginner's class at a different gym. I cannot tell you how hard it was to watch my daughter on the first day of her new class. I gritted my teeth as she somersaulted and cartwheeled down the mat with her friends. My seven-year-old daughter, who could do ten back handsprings in a row, was a "beginner." But more important, she was a kid again. Seeing her smile and hearing her laugh, I knew I had made the right choice.

Today she is on the varsity cheerleading squad at her high school and loving every minute of it. She is not going to the Olympics, but she is participating in a sport that she enjoys. And, unlike her mother, her status as a cheerleader does not define her worth. Sure, she would be disappointed if she didn't make the squad, but she wouldn't be left feeling worthless.

Fortunately, my painful lesson with my daughter helped me to ease up on my sons when it came to their involvement in sports. My youngest son, Hayden, puts enough pressure on himself to perform. All he needs is a mom (or dad) screaming at him from the sidelines or grumbling in the stands. He will berate himself for fumbled balls, bad pitches, missed catches, or pop flies. When he does, I calmly remind him that his worth is not defined by what he does or does not do. On the flip side, there have been many games where he has been awarded the coveted team ball, and I have had to remind him that worth is not defined by our successes. Does this mean it's wrong to feel a boost of worth when we accomplish something? Absolutely not! There is a huge difference between recognizing our successes as a temporary boost to our esteem and seeing them as a defining factor to our self-worth. The latter will leave us empty and insecure when accomplishments do not come.

The false-worth formula "worth = what you do" is not just being peddled on the ball field or in the gym. I am disturbed by the obsession that many well-meaning Christian parents have when it comes to their children's academic achievements.

I recently overheard some young mothers comparing the curriculum offered by some local day cares for their one-year-olds. For heaven's sake! What's the goal here? Are they grooming them for summer internships at Microsoft by the age of twelve? When my kids were one, they played in dirt piles and threw their juice cups across the room. That was the curriculum! I admit to subjecting my firstborn to some occasional phonics flash cards, but I learned my lesson when he happily gummed them down to a gooey mess.

Many parents have reasoned that being smart will lead to good colleges, and good colleges will lead to good jobs, and good jobs will lead to money and success, and money and success will ultimately lead to happiness. While we should encourage our sons to strive for excellence and work to the best of their God-given abilities, we need to be careful that we do not send a mixed message that emphasizes achievements, a successful job, and financial prosperity as means to define self-worth.

Of what benefit are our sons to God's spiritual harvest if they graduate with honors, attend great colleges, and someday nab elite jobs but fail to understand their true purpose in life? We do our sons a great disservice if we lead them to believe that worth can be found in prestigious jobs that come as the fruit of good grades and higher education. While I desire to provide my children with a good education, my ultimate goal is to raise them to know that true worth can only be found by believing in Christ.

In order to counteract the world's formula of "worth = what you do" in our sons' lives, we must first make sure we have not fallen prey to believing the formula ourselves. Our actions will most certainly speak louder than our words.

3. *Worth = What Other People Think.* Perhaps one of the most commonly uttered phrases by a parent to their teen child is, "You shouldn't care so much about what other people think."

When our sons are young, they look to us, their parents, for approval. They want praises for the pictures they draw in pre-school or the towering castles they build with blocks. As they approach late grade school, they begin to look for approval from their friends.

From the silent places in their hearts they ask, *Do you like me? Do you accept me? Am I cool enough? Would you choose me to be your friend?* Unfortunately, kids can be cruel and the answers are not always kind.

Eleanor Roosevelt once said, "No one can make you feel inferior without your consent." What valuable insight for our sons and ourselves. If we are to counteract the world's formula that "worth = what other people think," we must be active in encouraging our sons to care less about what other people think and more about what God thinks.

And let us not forget that our sons are not exempt from being unkind themselves. The adolescent years are tumultu-ous, regardless of whether they come from a healthy home or a dysfunctional one. Boys who have not been given a proper foundation for establishing their worth will be especially sus-ceptible to peer pressures of every sort. Christians are not exempt from seeking worth through the approval of others. Surely we can all think of Christian adults who have yet to shed their people-pleasing tendencies and wear themselves out trying to get others to notice and approve of them. At times I still find myself affected by the opinions of others and have to make a concentrated effort to dwell on the one true formula for worth.

The process of becoming a published author has produced some of the most exciting moments of my life and some of the most humbling. My initiation into the Christian publishing world came with the release of my first book (and the counterpart to this book), *Your Girl: Raising a Godly Daughter in an Ungodly World*. It was written from a deep burden in my heart to inform mothers of what I had discovered in the trenches of today's godless teen culture and equip them to counter that culture. I knew I had been commissioned by God to write the book, and I took the job seriously.

The first time I saw the book on a shelf in a bookstore, I was overwhelmed by the reality of how difficult it would be for my book to actually make it off the shelf and into the customer's hands, to the checkout for purchase, and into the customer's shopping bag. There my book sat, with thousands upon thousands of other wonderful books, all bidding at the same time for the attention of each customer that passes by. I honestly didn't know whether to laugh or cry. (For the record, I laughed in the store and cried when I got home.)

While the measuring stick of success for some authors may be the cha-ching of the cash register and the royalty checks that follow, that's not the case for me. For the sincere author, especially the Christian author who has been commissioned with a message from God, the goal is that the book will be *read*. I knew that even if it were purchased, it would compete with crowded day-timers and other leisure activities. I myself had purchased many books with the good intention of reading them. Some I read, and others went unread. Many met their ultimate fate in a cardboard box, tagged with a 25¢ sticker and sold at the neighborhood garage sale years later. As I saw my book on the store shelf, I was overwhelmed with the thought that it might not make it into the readers' hands and, ultimately, their hearts.

You can imagine how surprised I was a month later when I received word that *Your Girl* had made the Christian best-seller's list in the first month of its release (in the parenting category). Talk about doing the happy dance! I would be lying if I told you that it didn't boost my worth a tad. And then the e-mails from readers began to trickle in. My prayers were answered—my book was being read.

I gave God full credit and returned to writing my next book, *The Virtuous Woman*. But a funny thing happened with the release of *The Virtuous Woman*. It didn't make the Christian best-seller list. Sales-wise, it did *well*, but it didn't do *as well as* the first book. I began to berate myself mentally and at one point even questioned my calling to write. Somehow I had unknowingly retreated back to the familiar worth equations that had dominated my earlier years. I had linked the success and the popularity of my first book to my performance (worth = what you do) and the approval of others (worth = what other people think). Without even realizing it, I had set the bar high and made the best-seller list the benchmark for all future books. What had once been a "dream come true" (a best-selling book) had now become an expectation. And when the next book didn't meet my self-imposed expectations, I found myself questioning my worth. This private pity party lasted for several weeks. And the enemy was thrilled, cheering me on the whole way.

Much like the recovered alcoholic who falls off the wagon and is faced with the daunting task of getting back up and trying again, I, too, faced a similar challenge. God gently reminded me of my original calling to write—an assignment for him and for his approval alone. In the end and with his help, I reminded myself that it does not matter if a book ministers to one or many as long as I am obedient to the task he has assigned me. I write for an audience of One.

I have shared the above story with my children because I want them to see how pervasive the world's formulas for worth are: they will fight to take root in their very souls. I want them to know exactly *who* is peddling these formulas. If Mom, who writes about them and speaks on the topic across the country, can be ensnared by the lies once again, so can they. True worth does not come from a one-time revelation. It is a constant battle, every minute of every day, to wrap our minds around God's one true formula for worth. My sons will experience mountaintop moments when they will be tempted, just as I was, to get swept up in the world's formulas for worth. Maybe it will be a dream job, a promotion, or an award of some sort. Maybe they will someday be asked to be a deacon or voted onto a company's board of directors. If they have learned to define their worth by God's formula rather than the world's formulas, their worth will still remain, even if their house of cards comes tumbling down.

God's Formula for Defining Self-Worth

Worth = Who You Are in Jesus Christ. True self-worth can only be found by examining who we are in Jesus Christ. Our sons need to be taught that while the world focuses on outer appearance and defines worth according to "what you look like," God is more concerned with the heart and what they look like on the inside. When they come to terms with the awesome realization that they are fearfully and wonderfully made by the Creator of the universe, they will be able to stare at their reflections in the mirror and say, "I will praise you, Lord."

Our sons must be taught that while the world focuses on achievements and defines worth according to "what you do," God is more concerned with who they are. Try as they may, it will be impossible to earn God's acceptance by goods deeds. In fact, Isaiah 64:6 reminds us that "all our righteous acts are like filthy rags" to God.

The world often puts conditions on its approval, but God does not. Our sons must be warned that if they attempt to define their worth by what they do, it will only offer a temporary, fleeting satisfaction. There will come a day when they will grow weary of jumping through the world's hoops in order to earn yet another title, label, or accolade.

Our sons must be taught that if they define their worth according to what others think of them, they will set themselves up for heartache in the future. They will never find anyone who spends more time thinking about them during the course of a day than their Creator. In fact, Psalm 139:17–18 says, "How precious to me are your thoughts, O God! How vast is the sum of them! Were I to count them, they would outnumber the grains of sand." There's not a person alive who can hold a candle to that. Paul summed the people-pleasing tug-of-war when he said, "Am I now trying to win the approval of men, or of God? Or am I trying to please men? If I were still trying to please men, I would not be a servant of Christ" (Gal. 1:10). Who would reject the one true formula for defining worth and settle for the world's formulas? Only someone who has failed to understand that God demonstrated his own love for us when he allowed his Son, Jesus, to die for us, even though we didn't deserve it. Romans 5:8 says, "While we were still sinners, Christ died for us."

Years ago, at a women's conference where I was the keynote speaker, I opened my message with this question: If you could be anyone in the world, who would it be? I shared that I had a framed picture of the person that I, personally, aspire to be. I held the framed picture close to myself so the women were unable to see whose picture was in the frame. I asked for three volunteers to come up and, one at a time, take a look at my picture to see if, by chance, it was the same person they aspire to be. One at a time I allowed each woman to take a peek at the picture. One at a time, each one shook her head back and forth indicating that picture in the frame was not the person she had chosen. I then held up the picture for all to see. It was a framed mirror.

How sad that so few people, if given a choice, would choose to be *themselves*. I want to raise my sons and daughter to resist the world's formulas for defining worth. I want them to define their worth by the only standard that matters—God's. Finally, I want them to find contentment in being exactly who God created them to be. He's crazy about them.

CHAPTER 7

Babylon: Will Your Boy Bow Down?

I will never forget a story a mother shared with me at an out-of-town speaking engagement. It involved a challenge her teenage son had recently faced. He was new in town and had just started high school. A few weeks into school, he heard on the announcements that "See You at the Pole" was scheduled the following week on Wednesday morning. He marked his calendar and looked forward to the possibility of meeting other Christians at his school. ("See You at the Pole" is a nationally recognized, student-led event that happens once a year. Christian students gather around the flagpole in front of their respective schools and pray on the designated morning before school begins. In 2004, more than two million teenagers in all fifty states met for "See You at the Pole.")

The morning of the event arrived, and this young man showed up at the flagpole, surprised to find no one there. He was a little early so he waited for the other Christians at his large public high school to join him. Five minutes passed, ten minutes passed, and still no one came. Not that it wasn't busy on his campus; a steady stream of students continued to bustle past him as the time of the morning bell drew near. This young man was faced with a choice. He could shrug it off and join the rest of the students as they entered the building and headed for their lockers, or he could bow his head and pray . . . alone. My eyes filled with tears as this mother shared how her son bowed his head in humble reverence to God and prayed silently.

I wish I could tell you that the story had a happy ending and that other Christian students, upon noticing this faithful young man, stopped and joined him in prayer. Unfortunately, that's not what happened. In fact, some students laughed as they walked past him, and others even mocked him. But he persevered and continued to pray. Where were the Christians? Surveys indicate that over 80 percent of teens in this country consider themselves Christians, so where were they? When the mother finished her story, I couldn't help but wonder, *Would my son have walked past this young man? Or better yet, Would my son have had the boldness, like this young man, to pray alone?*

In 1 Peter 2:11, Peter refers to the Christians as "aliens and temporary residents" (HCSB). We have all wondered at some point what our place is in this world. Peter reminds us that we are simply "temporary residents." *The Message* says it this way: "Friends, this world is not your home, so don't make yourselves cozy in it."

Unfortunately, many Christians have gotten a bit too comfy cozy in the world, all the while forgetting that their time spent on earth is only a rest stop on the time line of eternity. As our sons grow older and are faced with situations that could compromise their faith, we must do all we can to equip them in advance to stand firm as "temporary residents" in the world. Far too many Christians today are nothing more than cultural Christians. Many talk their talk, but when it comes to walking their talk, forget it.

It will be a natural instinct for our sons to want to fit in with the crowd and conform to the culture. As mothers, we must raise our sons according to Romans 12:2, "Do not conform any longer to the pattern of this world, but be transformed by the renewing of your mind." We must teach them early on that

Christians are called to live in the world without becoming of the world.

When I think of a biblical example of teens who succeeded in the call to live in the world without becoming of the world, I am reminded of Daniel, Shadrach, Meshach, and Abednigo. After Babylon conquered Jerusalem, King Nebuchadnezzar ordered that some of the younger Israelite men of royalty and nobility be brought back to Babylon to be taught the language and literature of the Babylonians. Among these young boys were Daniel, Shadrach, Meshach, and Abednigo.

Imagine how these young boys must have felt after being abducted from their families and taken to a foreign environment. The boys were to go through a three-year training prior to entering into the king's service. The king ordered the boys to consume a daily ration of food and wine from his own table; but Daniel, Shadrach, Meshach, and Abednigo refused the king's food and appealed to the guard to have vegetables and water instead.

Vegetables and water! Have you ever been on one of those fancy all-inclusive cruises? The kind where you can order anything and everything on the menu? Now, stop for a minute and imagine saying no to it all. No to the lobster, no to the prime rib, no to the hot rolls with melted butter. No to the midnight chocolate bar! Could you do it? Could you sit at your little table in the corner and gnaw on your broccoli (no butter!) and carrot sticks (no ranch dressing!) while everyone else digs in? What prompted these boys to make such a huge sacrifice? The boys knew that some of the food was forbidden under Jewish law and that it might have been used in sacrifice to false gods and idols. Thus, eating such food would have been against God's will. To Daniel and his friends, it was a matter of conscience and something they felt would compromise their faith. It just wasn't worth it.

Most likely Daniel and his three friends were trained early on by their parents to put the Lord their God above all else in the world. Perhaps they had parents who were purposeful in training them to stand for what is true and right rather than conform themselves to the culture around them. But how many Christian teens, if put in the same situation, without their mom and dad looking over their shoulders, would do what these boys did? As mothers, our goal should be to raise sons who, like Daniel and his friends, refuse to sample the forbidden delicacies on the world's table even when we're not there to encourage them to walk away.

Unfortunately, this is easier said than done. Our sons are not exempt from temptations, and they will be presented with a banquet table of delicacies that bid them to come and taste. I was recently discussing this challenge with a dear friend who has teenagers of his own. He described this paradox beautifully, saying, "We live in a society that is at the feast and, by nature, we are hungry. To sit by on the sidelines and watch others enjoying themselves while we fast is hard, and that is what we are asking kids to do. We know that these delicacies will eventually turn bitter in the belly, but it's so hard to say no when your stomach is growling."

As mothers, it is our job to help our sons resist the temptation to conform to the ways of the world by drawing firm boundaries when it comes to possible exposure to ungodly influences. Case in point: In the process of writing this book over a nine-month period, I have had numerous rounds with my oldest son regarding the hot topic of downloading music or burning CDs for his friends. The truth is, most Christian teens have conformed to this trend, including for a time my own son. In his defense, he had honestly not grasped the concept that burning copies of his CDs for his friends was equivalent to stealing music from the artist. When I stumbled upon him burning a CD (music he had purchased) for a friend and pointed out that it was wrong, he initially defended his action with: "Mom, it can't be wrong—everyone does it." Hmmm, where did I go wrong? Because it was such a common practice, he jumped on the bandwagon without a thought to filter it through God's Word. I am happy to say that once he had the facts and weighed them against God's standards (How about "thou shalt not steal"?), he came to the obvious conclusion that it was wrong. Of course, I refrained from the urge to say, "I told you so."

I wonder if Daniel or any of his friends ever harassed their moms in their earlier years. Regardless, in the end, they would have made any mom proud. While the rest of their Israelite buddies pigged out at the king's banquet table, Daniel and his three friends stubbornly stuck to their vegetarian diet. They fasted while the majority feasted. And their commitment paid off. Daniel 1:15 says, "At the end of 10 days they looked better and healthier than all the young men who were eating the king's food" (HCSB).

Lest you think these boys would only be remembered for their bold stand not to eat the king's food, this was only the beginning. Shadrach, Meshach, and Abednigo faced the biggest challenge of their young lives when King Nebuchadnezzar issued a command for all people to fall down and worship a gold image he had erected. This was not your average gold statue. It was ninety feet high! They were given strict instructions to bow down when the musical instruments began to play. Further, the king ordered that anyone who refused to bow down and worship the gold image would immediately be thrown into a blazing furnace (Dan. 3:4–6).

Not surprisingly, Shadrach, Meshach, and Abednigo refused to bow down and worship the image. The king was notified of their disobedience, and they were summoned to come before him. He gave them one more chance to bow down and worship the golden image and reminded them that should they choose not to, they would be cast into the fiery furnace. He further asked them, "Then what god will be able to rescue you from my hand?" (Dan. 3:15).

Now stop for a minute and think about their dilemma. It is human nature to want to conform, yet they overcame that temptation to bow down to the image the first time the song was played. What a picture to imagine the three young boys standing throughout the entire medley of music while everyone else had hit the dirt, most likely at the first blast of the horn. What a shame they were the only three. Would you have remained standing during the first playing of the song? Would your son(s) have remained standing? I hope so. If you think you passed the test, hang on a minute. Now put yourself or your son(s) in their places the second time around. Ouch. If it's human nature to want to conform; it's all the more so to want to *live*.

I love the boys' response to the king's command when he gave them a second chance to bow down and worship the gold image.

> Shadrach, Meshach and Abednego replied to the king, "O Nebuchadnezzar, we do not need to defend ourselves before you in this matter. If we are thrown into the blazing furnace, the God we serve is able to save us from it, and he will rescue us from your hand, O king. But even if he does not, we want you to know, O king, that we will not serve your gods or worship the image of gold you have set up." (Dan. 3:16–18)

Now, if that's not radical faith, I don't know what is. Forget the music and send the orchestra home. No need to even play a chord; these boys had made up their minds. Further, they knew their God was capable of rescuing them, but they did not have the foreknowledge to know whether he actually would. They were prepared to die for God rather than reject him by bowing down to an idol. How about you? Would you still be standing? Would your son(s) still be standing? Most of us, had we made it through the first song still standing, would have complied with the king on the second go-round after taking one look at the fiery furnace.

King Nebuchadnezzar was so angry with the boys' response that he ordered the fire in the furnace to be turned up seven times hotter than normal. In fact, the furnace was so hot that the soldiers who threw the boys into the furnace were killed by the flames. Of course, there is a happy ending to the boys' story because they were brought out of the furnace unscathed by the fire. When the king called them out of the fire, he referred to them as "servants of the Most High God" (Dan. 3:26). In standing for their God, they were able to publicly give the one true God the glory and honor he deserved. Likewise, our sons should be taught to care more about preserving God's reputation than their own.

I vividly recall a conversation with my oldest son, Ryan, days after the tragic Columbine High School killings in April 1999. He was in fifth grade at the time of the tragedy and a fellow student had told him about one of the students, Cassie Bernall. The story had gotten out that when the killers asked this young lady at gunpoint if she believed in God, she replied yes.[1] Ryan asked me a thought-provoking question: "Mom, couldn't she have just lied and said no and then later asked God to forgive her." In answer to his question, I told him that probably a good majority of Christians would have said no to the gunman's question had they thought it would have spared their lives. If that question wasn't difficult enough, Ryan's next question will remain forever etched into my mind. He asked, "Mom, what would you want me to do?" Speechless, I was unable to answer his question.

Later that night as I tucked him in, I shared that I had thought more about his question throughout the day and had come to a conclusion. I told him that, as Christians, our goal should be to come to a point where we love God in such a way that we would be willing to die for him. I shared with Ryan that unlike Cassie who was only seventeen years old, many Christians live their entire lives and never come to such a place. With tears in my eyes, I told him that it was my deepest desire that should

I ever find myself facing the same question at gunpoint, I would without hesitation stand true to my God. I ended by telling him that it is my prayer that my children would also come to the place where they love God more than life itself and stand firm to their convictions.

If our sons are to stand firm for God in the face of opposition, we must teach them the arduous balance of how to live in the world without becoming of the world. If we, as mothers, have not come to terms with our own status as "temporary residents" in the world, we will have little impact on teaching our sons this truth. I fear that a great many well-meaning Christian mothers have allowed themselves to be molded and shaped by worldly influences and have sent a message to their sons that it is possible to be friends with both the world and God. James 4:4 is clear when it says, "You adulterous people, don't you know that friendship with the world is hatred toward God? Anyone who chooses to be a friend of the world becomes an enemy of God." Let us not be fooled; God will not play second fiddle in the life of a worldly Christian.

The Key to Resisting Conformity

How, then, do we know if we have been conformed to the world and are thus modeling to our sons a friendship with the world? The second part of Romans 12:2 holds the answer: "Do not be conformed to the world, but be transformed by the renewing of your minds" (NRSV). Renewing our minds involves filtering the world's influences through God's laws and standards. When we become Christians, we must develop a new way of thinking. We are called to surrender control of our lives to God. It takes a conscious effort to resist the temptation to conform to the world and, instead, conform to God and his plan. God was kind enough to leave us the Bible, his divinely inspired Word, which he intends to be our road map for living. When we develop the habit of filtering our thinking through

God's Word, we are able "to test and approve what God's will is—his good, pleasing and perfect will" (Rom. 12:2b).

The truth is, our sons will be shaped and molded by something. Unfortunately, the majority of them—whether they are Christians or not, will be molded by the worldly influences that surround them. It is of paramount importance that we, as mothers, abide by Romans 12:2 and, in turn, raise our sons to abide by Romans 12:2. Without the realization that Christians are called to be "temporary residents" in the world, our sons will conform by default to the popular opinion of the day rather than to God's standards.

A recent Barna survey revealed that only 4 percent of teens look to the Bible when making moral decisions in life. A whopping 83 percent said they would make moral decisions based on "whatever feels right at the time."[2] In light of this survey, mothers would be wise to realize that a majority of Christian teens will not make moral choices based on principles set forth in God's Word.

I used the above survey results for a teachable moment when my son entered public high school. He had previously attended a small, private Christian school from kindergarten through eighth grade, so he was faced with the challenge of meeting and making new friends. His father and I have emphasized the importance of choosing appropriate friends to be in his peer group. I pointed out that (according to the survey) it is not enough to assume that just because people say they are a Christian or attend church, they will filter their moral decisions through God and his Word when faced with high school temptations. I further pointed out that out of the approximate six hundred students in his freshman class, it is likely that only 4 percent of students, or twenty-four students, will look to the principles set forth in God's Word when making moral choices. I forewarned him that just as Daniel's friends discovered, standing for truth may mean standing alone.

I am a reality parent, and I want my sons to know up front what temptations lie ahead so I can better train and equip them to stand true to their God. To illustrate this point, several years ago I warned my son that there would come a time when he would face the temptation to view pornography. I told him that it was not a matter of *if* he would be tempted to do so, but *when*. I cautioned him that many of his Christian friends would succumb to the temptation because many of them have conformed to the world. I also warned him that if the majority of his peers are making moral choices based on "whatever feels right at the time," be assured that their hormones will cast a sure vote to "go for it." I encouraged him to decide in advance to abide by God's standards and flee sexual immorality (1 Cor. 6:18) by refusing to view pornography.

Our sons must be taught to embrace the truth that there are moral absolutes, standards for determining right and wrong. The youth of today embrace the lie of moral relativism that says, "What's wrong for you may not be wrong for me, and what's right for you may not be right for me." Under moral relativism there is no objective standard of right and wrong. Instead, determining right from wrong is a subjective decision that varies from person to person.

Who can forget the big news story several years ago about Madonna and Britney Spears lip-locking on an MTV awards show? Do you know what Madonna had to say in reference to the kiss days later in an interview? "We're bored with the concept of right and wrong." Moral relativism at its finest. Madonna is making up the rules for her version of "right and wrong" and subjecting our teens to her doomed experiment on live television. And believe me when I say she is one of many who have an active agenda to blur the lines that separate right from wrong.

Popular Christian speaker and author Josh McDowell says in his book *Beyond Beliefs to Convictions* that "our kids need to see our lives as living examples of the wisdom and practicality of a life that is built on biblical principles of right and wrong."

He further says, "Most of our kids and many adults, as well, have bought into a cultural mind-set that says we work out our lives independently of God's absolute standards of right and wrong."[3] McDowell points out that this approach does not work in the real world and that living lives based on God's absolute standards is what works.

What Is Your Worldview?

To possess a belief in absolute moral truths created by God is to possess a biblical worldview. Everyone has adopted a worldview, whether they realize it or not. A worldview is a perspective on all of life. It is the lens through which one views the world-at-large and, thus, determines one's value system. The process by which one determines right and wrong is at the core of a person's worldview.

Unfortunately, many Christian teens do not possess a biblical worldview. The Nehemiah Institute has tested teens since 1988 to determine their worldviews. The PEERS Test measures understanding in Politics, Economics, Education, Religion, and Social Issues (PEERS). Results from each category are classified into one of four major worldview philosophies: Christian Theism, Moderate Christian, Secular Humanism, or Socialism.

From 1988 to 2000, the average scores of students in Christian schools dropped by 30.3 percent and now fall in the top half of secular humanism. Results of evangelical family students in public schools dropped 36.8 percent. The average scores of Christian students attending public schools now regularly fall in the bottom half of secular humanism, just above socialism. The Nehemiah Institute has determined that based on projections using the decline rate for Christian students, the church will have lost its posterity to hard-core humanism between 2014 and 2018. Further, they state that it will be the end of America as we have known it for over two hundred years.[4]

It is time for a remnant of Christians to emerge who, like Daniel and his friends, have learned the precarious balance of living in the world without becoming of the world. Unfortunately, just as Daniel and his friends discovered, the godly way may also be the lonely way. Daniel's refusal to conform to the world's standards did not hinder him from being promoted through the ranks of Babylonian government. Daniel 6:3 says, "Now Daniel so distinguished himself among the administrators and the satraps by his exceptional qualities that the king planned to set him over the whole kingdom." But the story does not end there. There were some who envied Daniel and set out to find grounds for charges against him. Daniel 6:5 states, "Finally these men said, 'We will never find any basis for charges against this man Daniel unless it has something to do with the law of his God.'" They petitioned the king to issue a decree that anyone who prays to any god or man over the next thirty days other than the king should be thrown into the lion's den. Further, they convinced the king to put the decree in writing, thus making it irrevocable. Read the Scripture that follows to discover whether Daniel conformed to the culture that opposed his faith:

> Now when Daniel learned that the decree had been
> published, he went home to his upstairs room where
> the windows opened toward Jerusalem. Three times a
> day he got down on his knees and prayed, giving thanks
> to his God, just as he had done before. (Dan. 6:10)

I love it! With the windows opened toward his homeland, he prayed and gave thanks "as he had done before." What many do not realize is that some seventy years had passed since Daniel was abducted from his homeland as a young lad and taken into captivity by the Babylonians. He was now an elderly man faced with a life-or-death situation. Imagine how easy it would have been to try to justify not bowing down for just thirty days! At a minimum, it would be tempting at least to close your windows and pray out of sight of the public eye! Lion's den or no, Daniel didn't give it a second thought. He simply did what had come naturally for him to do after all these years, and he went before his God. When word got back to the king that Daniel had defied the decree and bowed to his God, the king made every effort to save him in spite of his written decree. It was to no avail as the decree was irrevocable, and the king was forced to throw Daniel into the lion's den. In doing so, he said to Daniel, "May your God, whom you serve continually, rescue you!" (Dan. 6:16). God did, in fact, rescue Daniel by sending an angel to shut the mouths of the lions. Daniel emerged from the pit unharmed, and justice was served when the men who conspired against him were themselves thrown into the lion's den.

If we desire to raise sons who, like Daniel and his friends, do not conform to the standards of our culture, we as mothers must also refuse to conform. Like Daniel, we must serve our God "continually." The Hebrew word for "continually" is *tedi-yra'* (ted-ee-raw'), which in its original sense means enduring, permanence, or constantly.[5] Do you live according to God's Word consistently and with permanence, or does your commitment fluctuate such that you at times conform to the culture-at-large? What about your son(s)?

If after reading this chapter you have come to the sobering realization that you and/or your son(s) have conformed to the standards of the culture and have strayed from a biblical worldview, do not be discouraged. It is never too late to get back on track. It will take hard work and effort, but it will be well worth it in the end. If you have gotten off track, talk to your son and humbly and honestly confess to him (and God) your sin of conformity to the world and share your heart's desire to change. If he is in middle school or older and has grown accustomed to loose boundaries regarding the influences of the culture, you can count on resistance. The older he is, the more attached he will be to the world. New boundaries will need to be set to protect him from the influences of the culture and, thus, further temptation to conform to it. Persevere, and remember, you are called to be his mother *first* and *then* his friend!

The golden idol of secular humanism has been erected. Many of God's children have joined the ranks of the majority who will bow down to it on a daily basis. I want to raise my sons to abide by God's absolute standards and serve him continually. Our world is in desperate need of "Daniels." May our sons be among the remnant of Christians who will stand for God and his standards, even if it means standing alone.

CHAPTER 8

Surviving a Sex-Obsessed Culture

One evening during a long layover after an out-of-town speaking engagement, I was waiting at my gate and participating in one of my favorite pastimes: people watching. On this particular evening, a group of college students caught my attention. Their jackets and bags clued me in that they were part of the track team. They were in a world of their own, laughing and in good spirits.

About the time I was ready to turn my people-watching attention to someone else, I noticed a couple of guys and girls from their group walk up with plastic bags of drinks, junk food, and magazines. They dumped it all in the middle of the floor in front of their cluster of chairs, and—to my shock— there were at least four porn magazines. I'm not talking *Maxim* here. They had the hardcore stuff: *Playboy, Penthouse,* and the like. Once they got grabbed up (by girls and guys equally), they proceeded to thumb through them *together.* As if that wasn't shocking enough, their comments would make most anyone from my generation blush. One girl said, "I wish I had boobs like that." A guy jokingly responded, "Yeah, me too!" (laughter) They held nothing back in their comments. They used every filthy word in the book.

What was most amazing to me was their cavalier attitude and total disregard for others around them—others like myself who didn't wish to be subjected to their crass talk and public viewing of porn. There was not a single student in the group who appeared to be uncomfortable and not one who walked away from the temptation. They acted as if what they were doing was perfectly normal. Mind you, these were clean-cut, average-looking college kids. They looked like they could be members of the average church youth/college group. I got up and relocated to the opposite side of my gate. As I sat there with a heavy heart, I wondered how my sons and my daughter would have reacted if they had been a part of this group. Would they have said something? Would they have walked away? Or by the time they get to college, would they be as desensitized as these students were to viewing sexual images and bantering back and forth about them inappropriately? I couldn't imagine it, but I couldn't help but wonder how many of these kids had grown up in the church.

Today's teen culture is obsessed with sex. The more entrenched I become in youth culture, the more shocked I am at just how bad it really is and how much worse it is becoming. From the moment they wake up to the moment they go to bed, they are inundated with numerous sexual images and references to sex. I must admit, as a parent of teens, I sometimes wonder if it's even possible to protect them from the media messages that rob the innocence of our children for the sake of making a buck.

Let me warn you in advance that some of the information presented in this chapter will depress you. I struggled in writing it because the research and studies support the fallout I am already witnessing among our Christian youth today. While some of this information may leave you feeling as if it is a hope-less situation, let me be quick to remind you that God has equipped us with everything we need to counter the culture. It will take much effort on our part, but we must step up to the plate and be aware of what our preteens and teens are up against.

Before I dive in and give you an overview of our sex-saturated culture, let me first address some basic assumptions that many Christian mothers make prior to (or during) the teen years. I was personally guilty of all three of the assumptions and was caught completely off guard when my kids hit the teen years. Unless these common assumptions are addressed, it will be impossible to respond or react adequately to the negative influences our sons will be exposed to. Notice I said "will be exposed to" rather than "could be exposed to." That is the first assumption we will need to address.

False Assumption 1: With careful attention and appropriate boundaries in place, I can fully protect my son from damaging influences.

Guess what? That sounds just like I did before my son hit the teen years! When he did, it quickly became clear that short of packing up and moving the family to the nearest Amish community, it would be impossible to protect him. And before you decide to consider the Amish route and outlaw all forms of technology, you might be interested to know that it is not uncommon for Amish teens to sow their oats before officially "joining the church"!

If you have adopted assumption number one as your mantra, please know that it is not my intent to dash your hopes of protecting your son's purity. *I was you*. I was quick to pass judgment on many Christian moms of teens whom I had determined were wimps when it came to drawing firm boundaries in the sand. That is, until my own kids entered the teen years. Oh boy, was I ever blindsided by the constant barrage of negative influences coming from various media sources. My comfortable Dobson-esque parenting formulas that had served me well in the toddler and grammar school years had suddenly expired. I was in the big leagues now. I found myself in an uphill battle to preserve the purity of my teens, and the deck was stacked against me. It was as if my husband and I were starting over from scratch. Many of my well-meaning never-evers uttered in the earlier years now rang hollow in my ears. "I will never ever allow my teenager to IM." "I will never ever allow my teenager to have a cell phone." "I will never ever allow my teenager on the computer when I'm not home." "I will never ever allow my teenager to watch a PG-13 movie." "I will never ever allow my teenager to go out with a girl."

You would surely think I would have remembered my lesson of proclaiming premature never-evers back when my kids were younger. "I will never ever allow my child to have a pacifier." (Said during first pregnancy. All three of my kids had a pacifier until the age of three.) "I will never ever put my child to bed with a bottle." (Followed through on the first two kids but blew it on the last one. And go figure—he's the only one who doesn't need braces.) "I will never ever let my toddler sleep in my bed." (My second child caused me to recant. Did you know that sleep deprivation was commonly used as a form of torture on prisoners in times of war as an attempt to obtain sensitive information? If there's a way out, take it!) "I will never ever send my kids to public school." (My two older kids attend public school.)

Now when I hear mothers of younger kids mutter the same never-evers in regard to the teen years, I just smile and say, "Never ever say 'never ever.'" We can draw boundaries, but we can't fight every battle. If we do, we can expect a rebellion by our sons somewhere down the road. There is no detailed parenting manual that gives clear-cut instructions when it comes to raising our teenage sons to live *in* the world without becoming *of* the world. As moms, we must go before God and find the formula that works best for each one of our sons. We *will* make mistakes along the way. The key is to be engaged in our sons' lives; stay in constant communication with God, who knows them best; establish appropriate boundaries; and pray a hedge of protection around their hearts.

False Assumption 2: My son will not be exposed to damaging influences of a sexual nature because he (fill in the blank): is involved in the youth group/goes to a Christian school or is homeschooled/is a committed Christian, etc.

The truth is, no one is exempt from being exposed to harmful influences. While there may be certain settings (church, Christian school, etc.) that lend to your son's moral development by teaching him to make godly choices, they will not be able to completely safeguard your son from outside influences altogether. In fact, the findings of many of the studies I will cite later in this chapter indicate that there is little distinction among Christian and non-Christian teens when it comes to sexual temptations.

This point was recently proven when I went to a popular teen Web site called myspace.com, which claims to be an "online community that lets you meet your friend's friends." The site allows you to create a private community where you can share photos, journals, and interests with a network of friends. While the site cautions against uploading inappropriate images, one glance at the site indicates that there are few rules being enforced. I was tipped off to the site by a concerned mother who shared a heartbreaking story about a "good" girl in their youth group who had up-loaded inappropriate pictures of herself on the site. She informed me that it was the new rage among the teens in her state to create profiles with pictures and journals. She went on to say that when the word got out about the girl in the youth group, most parents had absolutely no idea that such a forum existed. Many were further shocked to discover their own kids on the site.

Out of curiosity, I logged onto the site, created an identity, and ran a group search by plugging in the name of the high school where my own kids attend. While I didn't find profiles for my kids on the site (they know better!), I did find many of their friends. Most were innocent enough and highlighted their interests in sports, favorite movies, random thoughts, and such. I was proud of myself for figuring out the system, so I went a step further and decided to plug in the name of a different high school, the one where most of the youth at my church attend. And, lo and behold, if I didn't find youth from my own church! Some profiles and pictures were appropriate and some were not. In some of their journals (blogs), students from our youth group wrote of their weekend drinking adventures, and many confessed on their profile with a yes when asked about drinking and smoking. Ironically, many also filled in "Christian" on the profile when asked about religion. What a witness!

Some of the girls posted pictures of themselves in swimsuit tops posing seductively, and some of the boys posed shirtless while flexing their muscles (oh please!). Some kids had more than one hundred friends with their respective thumbnail pictures that they had added to their home page. Some of the thumbnail pictures were of girls baring cleavage or posing in thong underwear. The comments entered by others on some of our students' pages (some true friends and some new friends) offered a wealth of information into the inner lives of many Christian teens. Many comments were sexually graphic and loaded with offensive language. What really struck me was the cavalier and carefree attitudes that many of the students displayed on the site. It was as if they never imagined an adult could penetrate their private online world. Yet there it was, public information for all to see. I hope they don't run for public office someday! Allegations about draft-dodging and smoking marijuana won't even make the radar screen years from now!

There is no doubt that youth groups, Christian schools, homeschooling, Christian camps and events, and other like-minded Christian-based groups can have a positive impact on our sons. Yet we would be wise to remember that, while they may delay our sons' exposure to negative influences, they will not eliminate such influences altogether. As moms, we can never let our guard down when raising our sons. It is always good to remember that Christian organizations are made up of sinners. Where sinners are present, sin is not far away.

Generation Media

I remember when I was in high school that one of my friend's mothers complained because the DJ played Rod Stewart's "Tonight's the Night" at a school dance. Fast-forward to today, and that song seems pretty tame. Most teens (including Christian teens) have probably heard 50 Cent's song "Candy Shop" (Billboard Top 40 song). Take a look at the chorus:

> *I take you to the candy shop,*
> *I'll let you lick the lollypop*
> *Go 'head girl, don't you stop*
> *Keep going 'til you hit the spot.*[1]

Shocked? Don't be. The rest of the song was too lewd to put in print. What's even more shocking is the number of Christian teens who probably have a 50 Cent CD or have downloaded their suggestive songs and others like them onto their iPods or MP3 players. Many Christians alternate back and forth between their Christian music and their *anything but* Christian music. Some have given up on Christian music altogether. But it's not just the music that has influenced this sex-crazed culture. Add this to MTV videos that are nothing more than simulated sex; the prime-time sitcoms geared to teens where everyone is, in fact, doing it; the scantily dressed girls displayed in ads and elsewhere; and movies geared to teens that portray them as sex-starved junkies. It's enough to make you want to start a weekly rapture practice in your home. Our culture is out of control, and many parents feel helpless or have just reconciled that there's little they can do.

In the course of a year, the average adolescent will see nearly fourteen thousand sexual images.[2] *Playboy* magazine recently announced that it will offer galleries of photographs that can be viewed on digital media players. They will call their product "Ibod."[3] (Now isn't that cute?) Not worried because your child doesn't own an iPod? Well, porn is also on its way to cell phones. A Boston-based research firm said the mobile adult-services market would reach one billion dollars by 2008, and five billion dollars by 2010. One company, Brickhouse Mobile, is working with film studios and cell phone carriers to deliver adult content in the form of ring tones, wallpaper, video, and games—all downloadable directly to cell phones. They are quick to point out that they are working with carriers to develop standards and procedures for verifying the age of its customers.[4] Whew! I know I feel better; don't you? We certainly know how successful screening ages has been on the Internet! I wonder if they also have a plan for ensuring that our kids are not subjected to streaming porn clips while unknowingly standing near some pervert in a public place.

One survey indicated that over 70 percent of teens get their information about sex from the media.[5] When it comes to media access, teens log almost as many hours as the average adult does in a full-time job. A new study from the Kaiser Family Foundation that focuses on teens and the media says they spend over six hours a day engaged with some type of media, and that during more than a quarter of that time they use more than one medium at a time. They refer to it as "media multitasking." The latest results indicate that teens have become adept at media multitasking, where they access various forms of media at the same time. It is not unusual for a teen to be researching online for a school project while IMing their friends and listening to their iPods. For this reason, the generation of kids ranging in age from eight to eighteen has been dubbed "Generation M."[6]

The Kaiser study also found that:

- Kids' rooms have increasingly become multimedia centers, with two-thirds saying they have televisions in their rooms; half reporting they have video game players; 54 percent saying they have a VCR or DVD player; and 20 percent reporting they have a computer with Internet access.
- More than half the children said their families have no rules about TV watching.
- Another 46 percent say they have rules, but only 20 percent say those rules are enforced "most" of the time.

With so few moms drawing firm boundaries, is it any wonder our sons are imitating what they see in the media? In an attempt to lure prospective advertisers, MTV claims that it is watched by 73 percent of boys and 78 percent of girls ages twelve to nineteen.[7] It further tells advertisers that "young adults 15–17 are excited consumers and extremely impressionable. Now is the time to influence their choices."[8] Of course, MTV is influencing the choices of our youth with far more than products offered by advertisers. It has created an "anything goes" mind-set in the culture among our youth that has, in turn, produced devastating fallout.

The Parents Television Council selected a week in March when MTV airs a variety of shows highlighting spring break festivities. In 171 hours of MTV programming, PTC found 1,548 sexual scenes containing 3,056 depictions of sexual dancing, gesturing, or various forms of nudity; and another 2,881 verbal sexual references.[9] Let me break that down for you. There were, on average, eighteen physical and seventeen verbal references to sex per hour. Now imagine your son trying to sort through what he has witnessed. It is guaranteed to spill over into his real life as he becomes more and more desensitized to that which is exposed. To our sons it translates into an unrealistic portrayal of women as objects for sexual gratification. That alone is reason enough to block channels like MTV in our homes.

MTV defends its program content by saying it's a "mirror that reflects the culture."[10] While many may argue that MTV has "created" the culture, that is irrelevant. One study found that seventh and ninth graders were more likely to approve of premarital sex after watching MTV for one hour.[11] Unless we step up to the plate and assume responsibility for our sons' media intake and draw appropriate boundaries, we have no right to complain about the sex-saturated culture.

While my husband and I cannot protect our sons from every harmful influence that comes their way, we can be proactive and head many off at the pass by simply drawing boundaries. We block access to MTV and other like-minded shows. We do not allow our sons to purchase CDs or download songs with questionable lyrics. We do allow them to listen to the pop radio station, but if a song comes on that is inappropriate, they know to change the station or risk embarrassment when we take advantage of the teachable moment and launch into a lecture, often in the presence of their friends. We check out movies in advance on Screenit.com. They are not allowed to watch many of the popular shows geared to teens like *The OC*, *Life as We Know It*, *Desperate Housewives*, and many of the ridiculous reality shows. When it comes to their Internet use, it is closely monitored. (I will go into more detail regarding safe Internet boundaries in the next chapter.)

Most important, we have thoroughly explained to our sons the "why" behind our rules. I have heard my older son rib his friends over wasting their time watching shows like the ones mentioned above. He also abhors hip-hop and rap music and the immoral culture it breeds. He is popular, social, and likable, but he is generally not influenced by peer pressure. We have been purposeful in exposing the agenda of MTV and other media sources that take advantage of impressionable teens in an attempt to influence the choices they make. We have helped him make the connection between the media and our sexually promiscuous culture. Further, we have pointed out the fallout and long-term consequences associated with the fallout. We are not perfect parents, but our highest goal has been to raise our sons (and daughter) to view life through a biblical lens and filter the things they come in contact with through their instruction manual for living (the Bible).

Finally, brothers, whatever is true, whatever is noble, whatever is right, whatever is pure, whatever is lovely, whatever is admirable—if anything is excellent or praiseworthy—think about such things. (Phil. 4:8)

Caution: Girls Gone Wild

My two older children attended a private Christian school through eighth grade, and experienced a bit of a culture shock when they went to public high school. You can imagine how shocked I was to drop my son off in the morning and witness the various states of undress among the girls. My son had spent the last nine years witnessing his female classmates in uniforms. I was horrified when I overheard him talking with a friend one day about a girl in their algebra class who would "accidentally" drop her pencil on the floor, bend over to pick it up, and in the process flash her thong underwear!

But it was a pep rally I attended his freshman year that initiated me (and my boy) into this new world of girls gone wild. The drill team was dressed in low-rise jeans (the waistbands had been removed and frayed), white ribbed tank T-shirts (nick-named "wife-beater shirts"), with black satin bras and their bra strap hanging off their right shoulder. And that was just their costume! Trust me when I say that their dance moves matched their costume. The only thing they were missing was the stripper pole.

At that moment it dawned on me just how hard it is to be a boy in today's culture. Many of the boys cheered the girls on while dancing, and the catcalling that came from the bleachers left me wondering if I was in a gym or a strip club. While I was concerned for my own son, my heart was also grieved for these girls. Was their spot on this award-winning drill team so important that they would compromise their dignity? Shame on the drill team coach for prostituting these girls as objects. Shame on the school principal for allowing such a degrading display of sexual lewdness on school property.

And before we point a finger at the parents of these girls, I know firsthand of the politics that goes on in the home. No teen wants to be the only one on the team with parents lodging complaints. The coach and players often punish them if their parents come forward. My sophomore daughter just made the varsity cheerleading squad; and prior to her trying out, I politely asked the coach if they would be performing provocative dance moves during their routines. I was assured that they would not, but I am fully prepared to go to war should it become an issue. And before we point fingers at the girls for the sexual aggressiveness we are witnessing, let's remember that there are adults behind the scenes, not only condoning it but also *encouraging* it.

The reality is that there will always be girls who are willing to do whatever it takes to get attention from the boys. My sons recognize this and have been encouraged to steer clear of these types of needy girls. I have helped them make the connection that immodest clothing and promiscuity among girls are often signs of misdefined worth. Rather than take advantage of such girls, our boys need to see that it's nothing more than a cry for help on the part of the girls to be loved unconditionally. The challenge for mothers raising sons is to train our sons to respect all women, even the young women whose clothing and/or aggressive behavior invites disrespect. If we are honest, many of us can probably remember our own feelings of insecurity in our teen years. Most of us would be lying if we said we didn't at some point dress or behave in some way as to elicit attention from the opposite sex. It goes both ways, moms. Girls may invite attention, but many of the boys egg them on. Is your son one of them?

Hooking Up

One of the most shocking discoveries I've made in my years of ministering to college and youth students is that dating is all but obsolete. The old-fashioned "work up your nerve to call a girl, ask her out, pick her up, meet her parents, pay her way, and deliver her back to the doorstep" has been replaced by "hooking up," which involves sexual encounters with no strings attached. Some are arranged in advance among friends (called "friends with benefits"), while others happen spontaneously with acquaintances and strangers. One sixteen-year-old boy summed it up this way: "Being in a real relationship just complicates everything. You feel obligated to be all like, couply. And that gets really boring after a while. When you're friends with bene-fits, you go over, hook up, then play video games or something. It rocks."[12]

A 2001 study conducted by Bowling Green State University in Ohio found that out of 55 percent of eleventh graders that had engaged in sexual intercourse, 60 percent said they had done so with someone who was no more than a friend. The number would have been even higher if they had included oral sex in addition to sexual intercourse when asking the question.[13]

Oral sex among teens is on the increase, especially among the youngest teens. Surveys indicate that oral sex is viewed by many teens as a less intimate act than intercourse. One Arlington, Virginia, middle schooler explains it's "a sexual thing that keeps us from having sex."[14] According to Sara Seims, the president of the Alan Guttmacher Institute, kids have convinced themselves that oral sex "is not really sex."[15] An article in *USA Today* reported abstinence programs do not give a comprehen-sive approach to what teens should abstain from and commonly focus solely on abstaining from the act of sexual intercourse.

The article stated that experts cite many factors that have led to the increase among teenagers having oral sex. These factors include early maturation among girls, the media, instant gratification, freedom from pregnancy, the belief it is safe from disease, and the President Clinton–Monica Lewinsky scandal. One fifteen-year-old girl stated in the article, "The consensus in my high school is that oral sex makes girls popular, whereas intercourse would make them outcasts."[16] Physician and radio host Drew Pinsky has a Web site where many teens go to talk about sex. He is hearing from many young teens who engage in oral sex and consider it as "just a part of making out."[17]

Over the past several years, I have had mothers share heartbreaking stories with me concerning this epidemic. One story involved a fourteen-year-old captain of the cheerleading squad who performed oral sex on a boy in a hot tub at a party while her classmates stood by and watched. While speaking at a teen girl's event, another mother shared that the pastor of her large conservative church had received a shocking call from the manager of a local movie theater. The youth frequented the theater on the weekends, and the manager had identified them by their T-shirts bearing the name of the church. He expressed frustration to the pastor that his janitors were unable to get the semen stains out of the theater seats and asked the pastor to have a talk with the kids. It was a wake-up call for the parents of the youth. I am alarmed not only at the number of incidences brought to my attention but also the fact that many of the stories involve church kids who should know better.

The Truth about Virginity Pledges

According to a study by the U.S. Centers for Disease Control and Prevention, nearly half of all ninth through twelfth graders have already had sexual intercourse.[18] Approximately 66 percent of seniors in high school have had sex.[19] So your son signed a virginity pledge? Don't breathe a huge sigh of relief just yet. There is good news and bad news when it comes to pledgers.

The good news is that studies show that students who sign virginity pledges tend to delay sexual activity by an average of eighteen months. Unfortunately, that is also the bad news. Based on a study where over twenty thousand young people had taken virginity pledges in years prior, 88 percent claimed to have broken their pledge.[20]

Information like this is enough to make you want to throw your hands up and surrender. I'm sure many Christian parents, upon hearing this depressing news, are tempted to provide their sons with a box of condoms and the obligatory "God says to wait, but you probably won't be able to" talk. But also keep this in mind: A study by The Heritage Foundation has found that "teens who make pledges have better life outcomes."[21] The study further found that pledgers are less likely to become pregnant (girls who are strong pledgers are more than 50-percent less likely to have a teen pregnancy than are nonpledgers) and less likely to give birth out of wedlock. Teens who make virginity pledges will also have fewer sexual partners and are far less likely to engage in sexual activity during their high school years.[22]

I am a firm believer that the decrease we have seen in recent years of teens having sex outside of marriage can be attributed to the increased number of abstinence-based sex education programs in the public schools. We cannot afford to send a double message to our children by speaking out of both sides of our mouth.

Raising Boys Who Are Countercultural

It would be easy to think the battle is hopeless, but I was encouraged by a study that found that teenagers who "feel highly connected to their parents and report that their parents are warm, caring and supportive—are far more likely to delay sexual activity than their peers."[23] Additionally, another study indicated that teenagers in grades eight through eleven who perceive that their mother disapproves of their engaging in sexual intercourse are more likely than their peers to delay sexual activity.[24]

The National Campaign to Prevent Teen Pregnancy conducted a survey that questioned one thousand young people ages twelve to nineteen and 1,008 adults age twenty and older and found that 45 percent of teens said their parents most influence their decisions about sex compared to 31 percent who said their friends are most influential. Religious leaders were only the most influential among 7 percent, while teachers and sex educators stood at 6 percent and the media at 4 percent.[25]

And, moms, pay attention to this finding: 88 percent of teens said it would be easier to postpone sexual activity and avoid teen pregnancy if they were able to have more open, honest conversations about the topic of sex with their parents. However, the same study found that only 32 percent of adults surveyed believe parents are most influential in their teens' decisions about sex.[26] Moms, here is our hope. We have underestimated the power of our words, but our kids have spoken, and the verdict is in. We have a greater influence on the lives of our children than the media, but we must be willing to speak up! Given that bit of good news, let me encourage you to set forth with purpose in relaying the truths below to your son:

1. Your body is not your own; it belongs to God. First Corinthians 6:18–20 should be memorized by every preteen and teen before they encounter sexual temptation. It reads:

> Flee from sexual immorality. All other sins a man commits are outside his body, but he who sins sexually sins against his own body. Do you not know that your body is a temple of the Holy Spirit, who is in you, whom you have received from God? You are not your own; you were bought at a price. Therefore honor God with your body.

We should be purposeful in teaching our sons that virginity pledges are made to God and that they cover not only sexual intercourse but other sexually impure acts as well. I have spoken with many Christian teens who have justified that "everything but sexual intercourse is OK." One of the most commonly asked questions I receive from teens is: "How far is too far?" I share this answer: "Whatever you would feel uncomfortable doing if Jesus were present; and be assured, he is."

2. The majority of teens who have sex, regret it. Two-thirds of sexually experienced teens stated that they regretted their decision to have sex and wished they had waited longer before becoming sexually active.[27]

We need to let our sons know that many of them will experience peer pressure from their friends to have sex. We need to point out to our sons that it makes no sense to engage in an activity that brings a sense of deep regret to a majority of teens.

3. One in four sexually active teens will get a sexually transmitted disease.[28] Some STDs are incurable, and others can hinder or even prevent young women from bearing children. Remind your son that out of any given group of teens who practice abstinence, the number who will become infected by an STD is zero.

4. Nearly 40 percent of teen girls will become pregnant before the age of twenty.[29] Therefore, four of every ten teen girls will be faced with the reality of raising a child, placing a child up for adoption, or having an abortion. Often, boys are given little say in what decision is made and end up unexpectedly strapped with child support, the responsibility of raising a child, or the guilt that can come from terminating a pregnancy. Is it really worth gambling your future for a few moments of passion? We must teach our sons to think past the moment and consider the consequences.

As mothers, we have great power in influencing our sons to abstain from sex until marriage. We must clearly articulate to our sons that sexual activity outside of marriage is wrong and can have devastating physical, emotional, and spiritual consequences. We must also be quick to tell them that God created sex as something beautiful to be enjoyed in the confines of marriage. And whatever we do, we must not give up—even when at times it may seem hopeless.

As we near the end of this chapter, I have some good news for you. *Rolling Stone* magazine recently reported that there is a trend of counterculture teens emerging who are fed up with this sex-obsessed culture and are carving out their own niche of clean living. In an article called "The Young and the Sexless," this "new virgin army" finds their strength in their faith and the community of peers who have embraced the same values. Many of these teens have witnessed the fallout of this sex-saturated culture and are holding out for something better.[30]

My kids have been taught that the culture's anything-goes message regarding sex is a lie straight from the pit of hell. A lie that has already produced devastating fallout to a generation of teens and left many empty and longing for something better. I am not naïve. My children are not immune from stumbling at any given moment on any given day. But the longer they take a stand for God's best, the more they will feel that sense of accomplishment that comes from knowing they have chosen the good and pleasing perfect will of God . . . over a lie.

CHAPTER 9

Staying in Line
When Online

Remember back in the day when we would call friends and occasionally get that annoying busy signal? Or even worse, we were expecting an important call, and one of our parents or siblings was tying up the line. How did we survive such inconveniences? Average teens today need not worry. If they own a cell phone and a screen name, chances are, they can be tracked down twenty-four hours a day. On a recent family vacation, I was awakened by an annoying chiming sound in the wee hours of the morning. I traced it to my daughter's cell phone on the nightstand beside her bed. Unbeknownst to me, she had posted the following away message on her instant messenger account on our home computer. "Woo-hoo! On vacation at the beach! IM me!" She had programmed the IM messages she received to go straight to her cell phone as text messages. We had left the computer behind, but it still managed to follow us 750 miles across three state lines. Lovely. What about the word vacation did she not understand? I seriously considered hurling the gadget off our tenth-floor balcony into the waves below, but lucky for her, I opted instead simply to turn it off. Imagine that! What a novel idea!

I have a hunch I am not alone when it comes to my love/hate relationship with the Internet. As a writer, I could hardly

121

live without it; but as a mother, there are days when I've considered trying. In spite of my frustrations, I know the Internet is here to stay. To ban my sons from the Internet would be unreasonable considering computers are a vital part of their future. My option is to safeguard my sons as best I can by teaching them to be responsible and drawing and enforcing boundaries regarding the Internet. To be able to do so, we must know what is bidding for our sons' attention online and the dangers that face them every time they access the Internet. I am amazed at how many moms have adopted an "ignorance is bliss" attitude when it comes to their sons' time spent on the computer. Many of these moms exercised great effort in teaching their sons in the early years not to speak to strangers, give out private information, or wander far from Mom's or Dad's side. Yet every time our sons go online, they risk exposure to strangers, solicitations for private information, and with a few keystrokes, the ability to wander far from home—as in World Wide Web.

According to the Pew Internet and American Life Project, 81 percent of parents of online teens say that teens aren't careful enough when giving out information about themselves online and 79 percent of online teens agree that teens aren't careful enough when sharing personal information online. The study also found that 64 percent of all teens say that teens do things online that they wouldn't want their parents to know about.[1] But perhaps the most chilling statistic regarding the dangers of the Internet is that one in five children has been solicited for sex online by a sexual predator through e-mail or IM. One in thirty-three has been aggressively solicited where the predator attempted to set up a meeting with the child in person.[2]

We cannot afford to remain ignorant any longer. The good news is that you don't have to be computer savvy or break the bank to protect your kids from online dangers. Throughout this chapter I will discuss some practical ways to protect your sons from online dangers. In the meantime, it is necessary first to become familiar with the most common online activities among preteens and teens.

Instant Message (IM), Chat, E-mail

Instant messaging (IM) is the number one online activity for American girls ages eight to eighteen and number two for boys.[3] A marketing article addressing the online habits of teens notes that while many teens have their own cell phones, online communication reigns as the preferred method of chat. A Lycos survey showed that once the school day ends, 45 percent of teens preferred to communicate with their friends via IM outside of school, while only 15 percent preferred to communicate face-to-face with their friends.[4] The IM phenomenon caught most moms by surprise as we have struggled to catch up with the tech-savvy times. No sooner than most of us had mastered the art of e-mail, our sons had taken up IMing their friends. My initial response was to ban the practice from my home and insist that my sons resort to the old-fashioned method of communicating with their friends face-to-face or by phone. Of course, this reaction was based on my fear of the unknown, and once I came to the realization that IM would be a part of their lives once they left the nest, I concluded that I had a responsibility to teach them to use the technology in a responsible manner.

I am still on a learning curve when it comes to determining an appropriate age for extending IM privileges to my children. I did not have to address the issue when my older two children were in sixth grade as it had not yet caught on. However, this past year, my younger son (at the time, in sixth grade) asked if he could get a screen name and IM like the rest of his classmates. I decided to give him limited privileges—only after homework was done for about an hour before dinner but not on weekends. I sat him down and gave him clear boundaries such as never talking to people he does not know, never giving out personal information, never following links his friends send him, never accepting invitations to chat rooms, and only adding his close friends on his buddy list. The computer he used was in a central room of the house and, while I was not looking over his shoulder, I was normally in close range.

What my son didn't know at the time is that I had a software program installed on all our home computers that registers every keystroke made and sends a detailed report to my e-mail address of IM conversations sent and received, e-mails sent and received, and Web sites visited.[5] I could write a book on my observations of the IMing culture, and it provided me with more than a glimpse into this unknown world of instant communication. My original goal in installing the tracking software was to ensure that my children were protected from outside harmful influences. If someone was soliciting my child for personal information, speaking to my child in an inappropriate manner, or sending them links to inappropriate sites, I wanted to know about it so that I could take the appropriate actions to protect them. While many moms may argue that tracking devices such as the one I use are an invasion of their sons' privacy and illustrate a lack of trust in their sons, I am swayed by the fact that 89 percent of sexual solicitations are made in either chat rooms or IM.[6] It seems only responsible to spot-check our sons' online activities. We are responsible for their well-being, and while they live under our roofs, their privacy takes a backseat to their safety.

While monitoring my younger son's IM activity, I discovered much to my pleasure that he used the technology in a responsible manner. Unfortunately, I cannot say the same for other sixth graders who IMed him! Within a two-week period, he received an invitation from a classmate to visit a chat room that she claimed was "really funny." He did the right thing by declining, but the girl proceeded to recount in detail some of the things that were being said in this chat room. By her description it became clear that it was a masturbation chat room! Within days a sixth-grade boy who is friends with my son, IMed him and in the course of conversation made references to oral sex. Both of these children are from Christian homes and attend church regularly! In both situations my son did as I had told him and blocked the guilty parties from further conversation. Upon my discovery I had no choice but to sit my son down and inform him of the software. I commended him for doing the right thing but explained that in spite of that his innocence had still been robbed. I further explained that because other kids his age were not using IM in a positive manner, I could not risk it by continuing to allow him to IM. I told him that his father and I would reevaluate the issue when he entered seventh grade. It is a shame that my son has been penalized because of the irresponsibility of a couple of other kids.

We need to be purposeful in teaching our sons to think before they type. They are more inclined to type things they would never in a million years say to someone's face. I am shocked at the level of sexual banter that occurs through IMing. Ephesians 5:4 reminds us that obscenities, coarse joking, and foolish talk have no place among God's holy people. Fortunately, as more and more moms resort to tracking software on their computers, word has begun to spread to preteen and teen users. This has acted as a sort of deterrence as many preteens and teens think twice about what they are typing, knowing it is possible that a parent is reading the comments on the other end—if not their own! I have had to come clean with all three of my children about the software, and while they are not crazy about having their conversations monitored, they understand that my ultimate goal is to protect them from outside harm. One of my daughter's friends recently slipped and said a bad word in an IM conversation, only to follow it with: "Whoops, I'm sorry Mrs. Courtney!"

IMing, chatting, and e-mail are privileges that we should make our sons earn by demonstrating that they can be trusted to use it responsibly. I have allowed my sons to have e-mail accounts, but again, I am able to monitor (should I choose to do so) every e-mail that is sent and received. I have found that e-mail becomes less and less popular as the popularity of IMing increases. When it comes to online chatting, my kids are not allowed to enter chatrooms unless it is a private chatroom with their friends (much like three-way calling on the phone). While there is no foolproof formula for determining what age is appropriate for IMing, the software definitely gives you a means to better evaluate the issue and make an informed decision. You may choose a different standard for your sons (and daughters), but I encourage you to, at the very least, have rules and boundaries in place that you have clearly communicated to your sons.

Online Gaming

While recently en route to a speaking engagement, I struck up a conversation with a concerned father who was sitting next to me on the flight. He was on his way to help his twenty-one-year-old son pack up from college mid-semester and move back home. This one-time honor student had managed to flunk out of college due to an online gaming addiction. This father shared a heart-wrenching tale about his all-American boy, who had once played on the varsity football team in high school. He traded his college education for his obsession with getting to the next level on his favorite multiplayer game. Now he was coming home to live with Mom and Dad, find a job, and pick up the pieces of his life. (Of course, they had to install a software program on their home computer that would block their adult son from his online games until he could see a counselor and get some help for his addiction.)

Most of us with sons have experienced the world of gaming to some degree. As a mother of an older teen boy, I have witnessed the evolution from the basic Nintendo system to include SuperNintendo, Nintendo 64, GameCube, Xbox, PlayStation, PlayStation 2, and Xbox 360. From a mother's perspective I can't tell you the difference between the systems except for the annoying fact that the previous system's games usually won't work in the next system. My battles over gaming usually began in front of the television and progressed to the computer as the technology advanced to offer a means to play online with a network of friends (or strangers). No longer was it necessary to have multiple controllers—now you just go online and link up. With a headset you can even discuss the game with other players as you play along.

In addition to the concern about possible gaming addictions is also the concern about the violent nature of many of the games and its impact on those playing. It doesn't take a rocket scientist to figure out that countless hours spent shooting people up and watching their blood spill out onto the streets will, at the very least, leave a player desensitized to actual violence. In a report presented to Congress in 2004 to encourage stricter rating standards for games, the National Institute on Media and the Family documented the violent nature of some of the video games in question. The institute subsequently handed the game industry an F grade for the dramatic increase in violent games and, in particular, games depicting (and even rewarding) violence against women. The report went on to describe one of the animated games where the player scores points as a male figure gets into a car and has sex with a prostitute, then scores more points when he beats and kicks her to get his money back.[7]

Many of these games with "mature" ratings fall into the hands of children. If that's not bad enough, online versions of the games are not rated at all. The best way to curb potential addictions and monitor which games contain violent or sexual content is to limit the amount of time your son spends playing video and/or online games and be diligent about checking the ratings on the outside package. My younger son (now twelve years of age) is not allowed to play online role-playing games at all, and both my boys have limits on the amount of time they spend playing their games. I knew I had to take action a couple of years ago after my older son wiled away an entire summer playing an online game with a neighbor friend. At the end of the summer, he shared his deep regret over wasting his valuable summer vacation on the computer. The experience served as a much-needed wake-up call as he continually lamented that there was nothing he could ever do to redeem the lost time. To this day he is better able to monitor himself online and respect the time limits we have set. It seemed to make a tremendous impact on my son—not to mention his younger brother! I would much rather him waste a summer in high school and use it as a teachable moment in the years that follow than face the plight of the poor father on the plane whose son had failed to learn self-restraint before heading off to college. He wasted much more than a summer.

One article on the increase in gaming addictions noted the following psychological symptoms that could indicate an addiction: neglecting friends and family, feeling empty or irritable when not at the computer, and an inability to stop playing the game. The article further recommended support groups and therapy for those who are addicted.[8] Unfortunately, there is a lack of research in the area of gaming addictions and no professional standard for diagnosis or treatment. What that means, Mom, is that you are on your own when it comes to drawing appropriate boundaries for your son. Let me caution you against forbidding them altogether from playing their games. Nonviolent games played in moderation can increase their cognitive abilities and improve their hand-eye coordination. Not to mention, for many boys, it is a form of much-needed relaxation.

Blogging and Online Journals

In the previous chapter I introduced you to the concept of blogs with an account of the site at www.myspace.com. While it would be easy to assume that blogs are evil after reading my account of the myspace.com site, the concept behind blogs is not necessarily evil. In fact, the idea of people with common interests connecting is rather intriguing. There are many Christian blogs online that enable Christians to come together and discuss topics of interest. I should also note that I found some wholesome profiles on the myspace.com site. Some of the youth had used the site responsibly and had profiles that would be pleasing to God. There is no doubt that it can be used as a positive tool for exposing others to Christ, but it will not be without risks. I am not worried about my children posting inappropriate material but, rather, sharing too much personal data or being exposed to other profiles that are graphic in nature.

One detective in Plano, Texas, said that in five minutes of searching Xanga (a popular teen site used by many as an online diary), he found personal information about Plano children that a predator could use to get close to them. He said blogs quickly give predators information that would take weeks or months to gather from talking to kids in a chatroom.[9] Myspace.com even asks users to indicate their sexual orientation in their profiles. Add to the equation minors with inappropriate pictures and plenty of details in their diaries, and it wouldn't be hard for a predator or stalker to put two and two together and track down unknowing victims. For example, one fifteen-year-old girl listed her first name, high school, city, and state. She included in her photo album (visible for all to see), pictures of her posing in her swimsuit and cheering in her uniform at her school's football game. Even at a large high school, it wouldn't be hard to track her down. And this is only one example of many who openly shared the details of their lives for all to see! These teens are not thinking in terms of others who have malicious intent toward them. They are naïve and unreasonably trusting.

I recently read an account of a teacher at a private San Francisco middle school who discovered that many of the students were going onto the myspace.com site and others like it during school hours to update their profiles and blogs. This is what she discovered: "The students post their online journals, and the content is most alarming. They are uploading their pictures, lying about their ages, yet posting the school they attend, their birth date, what they do after school, places they hang out, discuss their sexuality—and the language is some of the most offensive I have ever read and they were updating journals during school hours. I can bet many parents and teachers do not realize how kids aged 10 to 13 have been interacting with these blog sites." She further said, "These sites are like a candy store for predators. Especially since the kids actually, truly believe that their journals are 'private.' They struggle with the concept that *nothing* is private about posting to the Web."[10]

The school ultimately printed out a hard copy of the profiles of each and every student who had used the site during school hours, attached a disciplinary notice, and handed it over to the students and their parents. When confronted with a hard copy of their profiles, many of the students were shocked and angry that school officials had viewed their pages on the site. One student even accused the teacher of invading her privacy! The students actually assumed that it was impossible for adults to penetrate their perceived private online world! *Perceived* is the key word here. Nothing is private on the World Wide Web! The teacher held a mandatory meeting for the parents. One parent naïvely responded to her information about the dangers of online blogs with: "Well, at least they're not out on the streets selling drugs," to which the teacher brilliantly replied, "Heck, being on the Internet is being on the streets, you just have to be able to figure out what neighborhood you want to hang out in!"[11]

Such is the world our children live in. Technology itself is not bad; some will use it for good and others for evil. Our job as mothers is to examine these influences and determine whether our sons will use it for good. We must also examine whether our son is likely to come in contact with those who choose to use it for evil and, thus, rob our sons of their innocence. You may decide that blogs like Xanga.com, myspace.com, friendster.com, and livejournal.com are acceptable for your son. However, I encourage you to go on the sites as I did and create an identity.

Surf around the site and run a search on your son's school. Find out where he is going on these sites, who he is talking to, and what he is talking about. These are the same questions we ask when our sons leave the house for an evening with their friends.

If you allow your son to create a profile and communicate with others in the network, have him show you his profile. Let your son know that you will be checking it to make sure he and others are using it in a responsible manner. Most importantly, remind him of the sobering reality that his information is not private. If the average mom can create an identity and check her son's profile in a matter of minutes, so can anyone else—relatives, teachers, neighbors, potential employers, friends' mothers, or predators. If they are truly looking for a spot to journal their most private thoughts, they might want to stick with the old-fashioned diary with a lock and key!

The Dangers of Porn

Imagine what Sodom and Gomorrah must have looked like prior to its destruction. Scripture gives an account of a place riddled with debauchery of every sort. In fact, Jude 7 notes, "Sodom and Gomorrah and the surrounding towns gave themselves up to sexual immorality and perversion." In Genesis 18:20–21, the Lord said, "The outcry against Sodom and Gomorrah is so great and their sin so grievous that I will go down and see if what they have done is as bad as the outcry that has reached me." Most of us know the closing chapter in this story. God, the Almighty Judge, examined the evidence and imposed a judgment by raining down burning sulfur on the two towns. Only Lot and his relatives were spared from God's sentence of destruction.

Each and every time our sons access the Internet, they stand at the gates of the rebuilt cities of Sodom and Gomorrah. It is a place where anything goes. In fact, some of the content you find on the Internet would likely make the people of Sodom and Gomorrah blush. So your son won't enter the gates of Sodom and Gomorrah, you say? The sad truth is that nine out of ten children ages eight through sixteen have been exposed to hard-core pornography on the Internet. Most stumbled upon it unintentionally while in the process of doing a homework assignment.[12] When my daughter was in eighth grade she had to do a report on a poet. When she entered the name of her poet into Google, up came countless links to lesbian chat rooms and sites. In researching her assignment, we discovered that the poet was homosexual, which likely led to the inappropriate links.

Internet porn is a $2.5 billion business. There are more than four million Web sites devoted to porn. According to Family Safe Media, a company that offers Internet filters and blocking devices, the average age when a child is first exposed to porn is eleven, and the largest consumers of Internet porn are kids between the ages of twelve and seventeen.[13] Twenty-five percent of boys polled by the Kaiser Family Foundation admit they have lied about their age to access a Web site.[14]

An article in the *Boston Globe* entitled "The Secret Life of Boys" spoke of a meeting with eight senior boys at a public high school and Boston-area psychologist Michael Thompson, coauthor of the best-selling book *Raising Cain: Protecting the Emotional Life of Boys*. He received a full show of hands when he asked the boys how many had downloaded porn. "More than 10 times?" he asked. Everyone. "More than 20 times?" All hands went up. "More than 30?" Unanimous. The article further stated this sobering truth:

> Adolescent curiosity about sex is normal. What experts fear about Internet pornography is the constant bombardment of violent and degrading images, which can skew boys' attitudes toward girls and can lead to earlier sexual behavior.[15]

By now we probably all know someone whose life was directly or indirectly impacted by an addiction to porn. Some boys and men are more susceptible than others to developing addictions to porn or compulsions to view it. Sadly, many boys believe porn is a harmless and normal rite of passage. As mothers, we must fight with everything we've got to protect the purity and innocence of our sons. The stats above may leave you feeling that it is a hopeless situation, but we cannot let that sway us from taking action. The key will be educating our boys to the long-term effects of porn. We must tell them the truth—that porn destroys marriages and tears apart families. We must tell them that it will leave them with an unrealistic representation of what God intended for sex. We must tell them that it is degrading to women and will impact their future relationships with women. Bottom line: We must scare them half out of their wits and leave them with the clear message that the fallout from viewing porn is so great that it's just not worth the risk.

My husband has taken my older son through the book *Every Young Man's Battle* and my younger son through *Preparing Your Son for Every Young Man's Battle*. I highly recommend both books. In the books authors Steve Arterburn and Fred Stoeker give boys and young men the practical advice to practice "bouncing their eyes" when they encounter inappropriate images or come in contact with scantily clad women. This is especially good advice given the immodest fashions many girls are wearing today, not to mention the unpredictability of porn popping up on the Internet unexpectedly. I went a step further with the authors' advice by pointing out to my older son that most women are more than aware of men who seem unable to "bounce their eyes" and instead practice the unwholesome habit of running "body scans" on women they come in contact with or pass by. I further pointed out to my son that the same is true for men whose eyes wander, even briefly, during conversations from the eyes to the chest. Again, women are aware of this, and it leaves them feeling devalued and disrespected. I told him that I personally am left wondering if the guy has a problem with porn since it is common knowledge that porn trains the user's eyes to view women as objects rather than people. It only makes sense that this habit would cross over into real life. This seemed to have a great impact on my son as it brought to life one of many long-term consequences of porn. What man wants to be thought of as a possible "pervert" by women?

We must also point out the impact porn can have on a future marriage relationship. Several of my friends whose marriages have been negatively impacted by their husbands' porn addictions had discovered in counseling that their husbands first began using porn in the high school or college years, long before they met them. In addition to causing fractured relationships, porn also causes a broken and distant relationship with God. God's Word reminds us in Ephesians 5:3 that there should not even be "a hint of sexual immorality" among God's holy people. The truth is, you cannot completely protect your son from being exposed to porn. However, you can equip him with the truth regarding its devastating consequences, train him to practice self-control by learning to "bounce his eyes," and put a filter on your home computers (more on this later). Finally, devote yourselves to prayer and be willing to trust God for the parts you cannot control.

Online Safety Tips

On a positive note, more and more parents are monitoring the online activities of their children. According to a survey by the National Center for Missing and Exploited Children and Cox Communications, nearly half of US parents claim to keep tabs on their kids' online activities, and 58 percent say they review what their teenagers are saying in chat rooms or instant messaging.[16]

Most parents are not familiar with teen online lingo. Fifty-seven percent don't know that *LOL* is "laugh out loud," 68 percent don't know *BRB* is "be right back," and 95 percent don't know that *POS* is "parent over shoulder."[17] The good news, however, is that you don't have to be Web savvy to stay up with what your sons are doing online and protect them from harmful influences. Here are five tips to help ensure safe surfing when your sons are online:

1. Place your computers in a central location where people pass by from time to time. Thirty percent of parents allow their teenagers to use the computer in private areas of the house, e.g., a bedroom or home office.[18] It only makes sense that our sons will be more cautious about what they are typing or where they are going online if they know that someone might be passing by their screen at any given time.

2. Install a filter on all your home computers! There are plenty of wonderful filters available. I personally use and endorse Safe Eyes, which is available for less than $50 on www.safebrowse.com. There is absolutely no excuse for not having a safety net of protection on our computers. If your son is one of many young men who will have a tendency to porn addiction, protecting him from inappropriate images that will otherwise stay forever imbedded in his mind is priceless.

3. Caution your son against giving out personal information and remind him that nothing is private on the World Wide Web. Explain the dangers associated with sharing too much personal information in online journals, chat rooms, IM, and e-mail. Encourage your son to look over what he is typing before he submits or sends it and remind him that there is a high likelihood that it will be viewed by other parties, including parents! Always explain the "why" behind your online rules and boundaries and explain that while you may trust him, you are not as trusting of others. We should never apologize for having online rules. Just as we have set up other rules for his protection, we should also do so with the Internet.

Educate your son about not illegally downloading music and files, as well as gambling sites. Be clear with your rules regarding what they are allowed to do online and where they are allowed to go. Consider posting your online rules near the computer as a reminder to your son.

4. Check your son's IM buddy list and/or profiles and comments on his online blog (if he has one) from time to time. Do spot checks on some of his buddies' profiles so you are familiar with the friends he is choosing to spend time with online. Your son can show you how to do this. Tell him that you will do occasional spot checks to ensure that he is not conversing with people who are questionable or would not meet with your approval. If one of his friends is in the habit of talking inappropriately or sends him inappropriate links, encourage him to block or remove him/her from his buddy list. I strongly encourage moms to have an additional software on your computers that will monitor IM messages and e-mails sent and received such as the one I mentioned earlier in this chapter. I personally use E'Blaster from spec torsoft.com and it sends me logs of IM conversations, e-mails, etc. . . . straight to my e-mail in-box. My kids are aware that I scan their messages from time to time as a protection measure.

5. Encourage your son always to come to you when he experiences something that is uncomfortable online. Surveys show that many kids will not come to their parents because they are afraid their parents will ban them from the Internet or withdraw some of the online privileges. Assure your son that you want to know when he stumbles upon questionable material and will not punish him for things out of his control. You must create a safe atmosphere for your son to come to you.

While we cannot protect our sons fully from harmful influences online, we can reduce the likelihood that they will be exposed to such influences by taking advantage of protective measures. Most important, we must be vigilant in teaching our sons about the long-term consequences of porn. According to industry studies, seven out of every ten men, ages eighteen to twenty-four, visit porn sites in a typical month. In the book *Pornified: How Pornography Is Transforming Our Lives, Our Relationships, and Our Families*, author Pamela Paul notes that when boys get to college, "Pornography is more than accepted—it's exalted." Without a hint of shame, some young men even leave notes on their doors that read: "Leave me alone, I'm watching porn."[19] This is the world in which our sons live. Before they leave the nest, we must prepare them for this sad reality.

As I mentioned earlier, I highly recommend a series of books for boys, young men, and men on the subject of sexual temptations titled *Every Man's Battle* by Steve Arterburn and Fred Stoeker. It should be required reading for every young man long before he leaves the nest. If you are a single mom or you are married but your husband is not willing (or qualified) to guide your son through one of these books, take the lead yourself. It may be uncomfortable at times, but the consequences that can result from failing to address this subject are far more uncomfortable. We must do everything in our power to raise our boys to, ultimately, monitor and protect themselves from the evils of porn. Far too much is at stake not to.

Part 3
THE HIJACKING OF BIBLICAL MANHOOD

CHAPTER 10

Warrior or Wimp—How Not to Raise a Mama's Boy

My mother had a great deal of trouble
with me but I think she enjoyed it.

—MARK TWAIN

When my son, Ryan, was little, I loved dressing him up in dainty smocked rompers and sailor suits with matching hats. His dad would groan and tell me that I'd be lucky if he'd ever speak to me again once he was old enough to see the pictures and witness this assault to his budding manhood. While Keith patiently tolerated the rompers and sailor suits during Ryan's toddler years, he drew a firm line in the sand one day when Ryan was four years old. While shopping in a fancy second-hand boutique, I stumbled upon an outfit fit for a little prince. It had a white pleated blouse with a sailor flap trimmed in Scottish plaid that came with a pair of black-and-white houndstooth knickers that attached to the top with plaid covered buttons. Add a pair of white knee socks and dress loafers and, voilá, you have instant royalty. As I stood there in the shop admiring the outfit on the hanger, I could picture my little lad hunting Easter eggs in the backyard while decked out in this finery. With that image I headed for the checkout.

When I got home, I put the outfit on Ryan so he could model it for his dad. When Keith came in the door after work, I had him stand at the bottom of the stairs and await the grand entrance of Prince Ryan. As Ryan descended the stairs looking every bit as adorable as I had imagined, his dad said something that remains a humorous family memory to this day. Without missing a beat, he said, "Honey, what in the world are you thinking? If he goes out in public dressed like that, his friends will beat him up." And then he paused and laughingly said, "Heck, *I'm* thinking about beating him up!" Of course, he meant it tongue and cheek, and Ryan, with a look of instant relief, rushed upstairs to change into his favorite Ninja Turtles T-shirt and sweatpants.

My husband, Keith, knew that knickers and knee socks are the wardrobe of wimps, not warriors. Fortunately, Ryan escaped my years of wardrobe abuse unscathed and, as per his father's prediction, Ryan is mortified when he sees the old pictures.

I would doubt that any mother purposely sets out to raise her son to be a wimp. Of course, raising a warrior is about much more than dressing our sons in the right outfits. As moms, we will play a critical role in developing the masculinity and strength of our sons with our attitudes and actions. What does it take to raise a warrior? Read on to discover whether you are stifling your boy's inner warrior spirit.

Warriors Are Not Couch Potatoes

Boys are wired for adventure. Tell a young boy not to play war games, and he will still figure out how to fashion a weapon from a stick on the ground or a celery stalk in his lunch box. Most moms can relate to Ralphie's mom in the movie *A Christmas Story*. The focal point of the entire movie is young Ralphie's obsession with getting a Red Ryder 200-shot, Range Model air rifle (translation: BB gun) for Christmas. The only thing that stands in his way is his mom and his mom's refusal and well-rehearsed mantra, "You'll shoot your eye out." Ralphie goes to desperate measures to change his mother's mind by placing an ad for the gun in a copy of her *Life* magazine, convinced that she will see the ad and suddenly come to her senses and realize the gun's role in his journey to manhood.

These scenes are not far from reality when it comes to the intense need boys have for action and adventure and the natural response of the average mother to suppress this need. My poor Ryan was subjected to constant reminders to "be careful," "don't run," "wipe your nose," "sit still," and "use your inside voice." When his younger brother, Hayden, entered the picture five years later, it became clear that I was outnumbered. I had no choice but to lighten up in the years that followed. Hayden was allowed to climb trees to heights that Ryan had never known, roller blade without knee pads, jump on trampolines without a spotter, and yes, even fall down and get hurt.

As a past overprotective mom, I have come a long way. I recently even took Hayden and one of his friends to a skateboard park. Watching him wipe out and barely get up before being pummeled by another skateboarder sent me to the waiting area to pray that the hour would end without a trip to the emergency room. My years of holding Ryan back were redeemed in the years that followed. I knew he was going to be OK when one day I pulled up in front of my house to find him (sixteen years old at the time) rolling down our steep one-hundred-foot driveway on an old office chair he had discovered in the garage. As if that wasn't enough to cause me to grab my heart, at the bottom of the driveway was a skateboard ramp with a pile of cardboard boxes on the other side, no doubt to cushion the blow. His friends (and younger brother) were cheering him on as he flew past them at rocket speed. It was too late for me to interrupt his plan, so I sat in my car with the engine running, ready for a quick getaway to the emergency room. When he got up from the box heap and limped back up the driveway, I casually swept past him on my way into the house and said, "Hey, if you're going to do that again, come tell me so I can get it on the camcorder."

Now I know as I write this that there will be some moms who are appalled at my laissez-faire attitude toward what many would refer to as "an accident waiting to happen." I am certainly not saying that we turn a blind eye to potential incidents that are life threatening, chalking them up as standard boyish adventure. I do not let up on obvious safety precautions such as my boys wearing helmets when riding their bikes or buckling up when they get in the car. My goal is to encourage moms to evaluate whether they go overboard in their attempts to protect their boys from doing things that are ingrained deep within their souls.

What harm could befall them should they wish to spend the majority of their summer nights in a tent pitched in the backyard? My husband posed this question to me several summers ago on behalf of my boys. I relented, and on the first night a hungry raccoon sniffed out their stash of junk food and entered the tent uninvited. At that point I made a plea to my husband on behalf of "God only knows what else is living out in the woods and waiting to get them," and he gently reminded me that such stories are what divide the men from the boys. *Yeah right*, I thought. *You take them in for the required series of rabies shots should the raccoons overtake them in their quest for a midnight snack.*

For the life of me, I cannot understand how my boys can possibly enjoy some of the adventurous things they do. Ryan came home from a mission trip this past summer describing a game he and some of the other boys had created late into the night while camping out on the floor of a school classroom. Mind you, I had spent the week wondering if he had enough bedding to keep him warm at night or if he was drinking enough water during the day while repairing roofs in the hot sun. So you can imagine my confusion to hear him describe how much fun this new game was, a game they had named Blackout Shoe Massacre. I won't go into detail except to say that it boiled down to collecting everyone's shoes and putting them in a barrel in the center of the room. The room was pitch black, and one person was in charge of hurling the shoes at as many boys as possible as they attempted to escape the "shoe massacre."

When he was done, I stared at him in total disbelief and asked the obligatory mom question of, "Where were the chaperones when this was going on?" He laughed and stated the obvious: "Mom, they were playing the game with us." I knew then it was a lost cause. A man's need for adventure is not relegated to his youth; thus explaining the participation of our youth minister and several other men (one, a founder and CEO of a high-tech company) I had previously labeled as "mature and responsible." And to think I had spent my days worried about him having enough bedding and water.

Stories like that have helped me to lighten up over the years. Deep down inside I suppose I would worry more if they resisted adventure in response to my pleas to "be careful." When it's all said and done, do I want to raise a *wimp* or a *warrior?* This emerging attitude prepared me for my boys' pleas for paintball guns a couple of years ago. It has helped me reconcile their need to organize gangs of neighbor boys for paintball wars in the wooded area behind our house. One of my neighbors even asked me if I was running an antiterrorist training camp in my backyard after spotting a group of boys dressed in camouflage, paintball guns slung over their shoulders, heading between our houses on their way back to the woods. The boys spend hours in the woods and occasionally emerge for a necessary drink of water, compliments of the spigot on the side of the house. Like feeding wild animals, I will throw out a bag or two of chips, and they are good to go for another couple of hours. At the end of the war and once my boys' warrior friends have gone home, Ryan and Hayden will compare their war wounds (bruises), beaming with pride over each and every one. It was moments like this that made me realize that my constant reminders to "be careful" were meant to protect my boys from the bumps and bruises of life, but in reality the bumps and bruises of life are badges on their road to manhood. Trying to protect them from getting hurt would, in the end, hurt them more. They are warriors-in-training, and sometimes warriors get hurt.

While the term *warrior* might appear to be associated with *war*, it is important that we not typecast the term *warrior* to be associated with achievements in sports, merit badges from scouts, or victories on a battlefield. My boys happen to exhibit their warrior spirit through sports and outdoor adventures, but warriors are not just athletes and outdoorsmen. Many boys will have temperaments and gifts that lend themselves to the arts, academia, or other areas of interest.

When I think of biblical examples of warriors in Scripture, I immediately think of King David. While David was remembered for his many victories in battle, we must never forget his humble beginnings as a shepherd boy. A harp-playing, sheep-tending youth who volunteered to fight the invincible giant, Goliath, he refused the king's armor and opted instead for his own simple tunic, a slingshot, and five smooth stones. He would only need one stone to take the trash-talking giant down and send the rest of the Philistine army running in fear.

David was a warrior, but his warrior status was not the result of his victories but rather his attitude. When he faced Goliath, he made the bold statement, "I come against you in the name of the LORD . . . for the battle is the LORD's" (1 Sam. 17:45–47). David did not fight the giant in his own power but relied on the strength of the Lord. David proved that the battle is not a physical one but a spiritual one. Was David any less a warrior prior to his physical battle with Goliath? No. David, the shepherd boy, was a warrior. David, the musician, was a warrior. David, who danced freely before the Lord when the ark of the Lord was entering the city of David, was a warrior. David, the literary poet behind most of the psalms, was a warrior. David's attitude earned him his warrior status long before he faced Goliath. Had he never fought a single battle he would have still been a warrior.

Our sons will likely not come face-to-face with a physical Goliath to overcome, but they will have defining Goliath moments throughout their lives. David did not abandon playing the harp after he defeated Goliath. It was a part of who he was, and it prepared him for who he would become. He did not run from adventure but relished in it. A warrior can play the harp, sing in an opera, graduate number one in his class, write poetry, attend culinary school, and so on, but he does not shy away from adventure. A warrior is an overcomer, and adventure will be his playing field. God has prewired our boys for adventure, and, according to their temperaments, it will be expressed in a variety of different ways. We must not hold them back from experiencing the thrill of adventure, whether it comes from fighting a paintball war, spending the night in a flimsy tent while hungry raccoons lurk nearby, or playing a game of Blackout Shoe Massacre. We must let our boys be the boys that God wired them to be, boys who will someday be men.

Warriors Are Not Coddled

If there was ever a lesson I have had to learn the hard way, it is that boys resist coddling moms. When Ryan played his first year of tackle football in seventh grade, I thought I would never get used to the popping and grinding sound that helmets and pads make when they collide with other helmets and pads. And then one day my worst fear was imagined. Some big Goliath who looked like he was old enough to shave knocked my boy to the ground. I was proud of myself for following the obligatory thirty-second rule before I leaped out of the stands and ran to my boy's side. I arrived just in time to hear Ryan say, "Mom! What are you doing? Never ever leave the bleachers—even if I'm dying! Go away, now!" As I returned to my seat in the bleachers, I heard another mother whisper to someone, "It's OK, it's her first child—she didn't know better."

It is a mother's nature to rush to her son's side when he falls down, and in the early years her son expects and desires that she be there. His expectation and desire usually will change over the years, but a mom's nature will tend to remain the same. As moms, we want to protect our boys from experiencing discomfort of any sort. To this day I recall a boy in my sixth-grade class whose mother would bring his jacket up to school if the temperature dropped during the day. I can still picture her waving the jacket in the air and yelling, "Steven, Steven, honey, mommy brought your jacket!" while we ran laps around the backstop at PE. By the time we graduated high school six years later, Steven was the same boy he had been in sixth grade: timid, shy, and anything but a warrior. But, bless his heart, he was warm.

As mothers we must resist the urge to coddle our sons. Coddling a son past his infant/toddler years can produce one of two outcomes: a son who is emotionally enmeshed with his mother even in his adult years (a.k.a. mama's boy) or a son who harbors bitterness and resentment toward his mother. In the book *Wild at Heart*, author John Eldridge has this to say about clingy, coddling mothers: "I've found that many, many adult men resent their mothers but cannot say why. They simply know they do not want to be close to them; they rarely call. As my friend Dave confessed, 'I hate calling my mom. She always says something like, "It's so good to hear your little voice." I'm twenty-five, and she still wants to call me her little lamb.'" Somehow he senses that proximity to his mother endangers his masculine journey as though he might be sucked back in. Ouch.

As mothers, we must make sure that our innate desire to nurture our sons does not thwart their progress on their road to manhood. Mothers must find the careful balance of nurturing their sons without coddling them. I am certainly not saying that we turn a cold shoulder to our little ones when they fall down or pass on the dysfunctional message that "big boys don't cry." I am simply warning against erring to the extreme of babying our sons in their premanhood years.

Warriors Are Not Timid

"And we urge you, brothers, warn those who are idle, encourage the timid, help the weak, be patient with everyone" (1 Thess. 5:14).

When Ryan was in kindergarten at a private Christian school, the headmaster would take the time to train the boys on the mechanics of a proper greeting. If he approached Ryan, he would extend his hand and say, "Well, hello Mr. Courtney. How are you today?" If Ryan looked down at the ground (like the average five-year-old), the headmaster would patiently and gently tell Ryan to extend his hand, look him directly in the eye, shake his hand firmly, and with confidence say, "Fine, thank you." When Ryan would do so, he would say, "Atta boy, Ryan—good firm handshake." It was a great example to me and proof that boys as young as five can learn to greet adults respectfully.

Keith and I continued to enforce this school rule of etiquette in our home, and to this day our boys are generally at ease when greeting and conversing with adults. Had we not remained vigilant in training our boys in basic communication etiquette, they probably would be like the many boys who stare at the ground and grunt disrespectfully when adults speak to them. While I realize that many boys may be justifiably "bashful," this does not mean we should allow it to be an excuse to respond to others with silence.

Ryan was my bashful child, and we had to work with him to overcome it. I recall a time when we came to a standoff over his bashfulness. He was about ten years old, and I had told him that we could rent a particular movie he had wanted to see. When we pulled up in front of the video rental store, I told him that I would wait in the car while he went in to ask if they had the movie in stock. He begged and pleaded for me to go in and would not budge from the car. I stood firm and told him, "Ryan, you have to learn to take care of things like this. This person behind the counter does not even know you. You have nothing to lose." Finally, he gave up, faced his fear, and went into the store.

I realized that because of his bashfulness, I had grown accustomed to communicating for him over the years, and now it had become an expectation on his part. I had effectively prevented him from learning necessary communication skills that were vital to his future. It was now or never. From that day forward, if he was looking for a particular item to buy with his allowance, I would have him take the initiative to call stores and find out the basic information. He was hesitant at first, but if he wanted the item badly enough, he would eventually break down and call. Today you would never know that Ryan ever had a bashful/shy side to him. Had we not recognized his bashful tendencies early on and made a concentrated effort to help him overcome them, I doubt he would have had the skills to go out and find his first summer job this past year.

If timidity is allowed and even cultivated in our sons' lives, it can breed a spiritual timidity over the years. If our sons are allowed to shy away from uncertainties, what will keep them from shying away from matters that require faith?

Do you recall the story of Gideon sending out his messengers to summon the warriors for a battle to deliver the Israelites from the hands of the Midianites? In order to make sure that there is no question that the Israelites would be delivered by the hand of God, Gideon is told by God to pare down his force of warriors so they will have fewer men than the Midianites when they go into battle. To make the first cut of men, God tells Gideon this in Judges 7:3: "Therefore, tell the people, 'Whoever is timid or afraid may leave and go home.' Twenty-two thousand of them went home, leaving only ten thousand who were willing to fight" (NLT).

No doubt, it would take a great amount of faith for the warriors to believe that they would prevail in the end, especially with fewer men. If your son were of fighting age, would he be among the remaining ten thousand who were willing to fight, or would he be among the twenty-two thousand who wimped out and went home? Without intervention by parents or others, timid boys almost always grow up to be timid men. Warriors have no reason to be timid and afraid; they know whom they serve.

It is my belief that our culture has hijacked many of the components of biblical manhood. They have blurred the lines of what defines a man, leaving our boys and men confused and suffering from an identity crisis of sorts. Many men have abandoned their roles as providers, protectors, and spiritual leaders. Families are falling apart, marriages are in shambles, and gender roles have been redefined. The fallout is great, and today we are experiencing a shortage of real men. If our sons are to be real men, we must first help them cultivate the warrior spirit within. We must prepare them for the battlefields of life and groom them to be warriors, not wimps.

CHAPTER 11

Manhood, Masculinity, and Marriage Redefined

Imagine picking up a *Seventeen* magazine and reading an article entitled "Read 'Em and Reap," where girls are encouraged to read books such as Walt Whitman's Leaves of Grass and the Holy Bible. Thumb over a few pages and read an article titled, "Can Homemaking Really Be a Career?" The text below says this in regard to homemaking: "It is living . . . filled with variety, exciting and challenging." Or how about a colorful feature strategically placed in the center of the magazine on "How not to get another prom bid." It offers timely advice including a warning against taking part in gossip. Sprinkled throughout the magazine are recipes, dress patterns, and even homemaking tips. (All this in *Seventeen* magazine, April 1946.)

On the cover of the April 1950 issue of *Seventeen* was a girl in a yellow organza dress sitting properly with her legs crossed daintily at the ankles. She is holding a flower in her lap and glancing bashfully at a handsome young man who stands beside her. They are not touching. A closer glance reveals that he is reading to her from a book of poetry. Compare this to the stark contrast you find in *Seventeen* and other teen fashion magazines today. Sample subtitles read, "22 jeans that scream nice butt"; "Swimsuit tops that tease and please"; "Make the first move . . . p.s.: He's waiting." And make the first move, they do. As the mother of two sons, I am shocked at the aggressive nature of many girls today.

I am the proud owner of quite a few copies of vintage *Seventeen* magazines. I love to look through them on occasion because they offer a stunning glimpse into a world unknown to me and a world long forgotten. The oversized matte pages bring to life what it was like to be a teenage girl in an era deemed "the age of innocence." Woven throughout the pages were the themes of honesty, faith, and purity. I feel strangely conflicted as I saw the multitude of advertisements for Lane hope chests, engagement rings, and sterling silver flatware. In one *Seventeen* issue alone, I counted ten ads for sterling silver flatware and three ads for engagement/wedding sets.[1] One ad for silver flatware reads, "You've chosen your pattern—you've bought your first piece. It's a symbol of the home you'll have someday."[2] Another ad reads, "Most girls start collecting Towle when they first begin to think of marriage and a home of their own, very often before they have met the man of their choice."[3]

By the early 1970s, the silver flatware ads and engagement ring ads had dwindled to, on average, one ad each per issue.[4] Today they are long gone and any mention of marriage with them. Articles extolling the merits of homemaking—gone. The assumption of purity—gone. The obvious respect boys had for girls—gone. The encouragement of faith—gone. The warnings against gossip—gone. In fact, the magazines today represent a culture that has strayed from its biblical roots and left young men and women searching for purpose and identity. Where did it all begin to take a turn?

The Sexual Revolution and Women's Lib

To understand what could possibly stimulate such a drastic downturn in values, it is necessary to turn the clocks back to the 1960s. Think tie-dye. Think Woodstock. Think hippies. Think sexual revolution. Most of us are old enough to have at least a basic knowledge of the radical women's liberation movement that was birthed in the early 1960s. The women's movement has been around since much earlier than the 1960s. Many don't realize that it originated as a positive cause that began in the mid 1850s. Some of the social reform groups that grew out of these efforts included the Abolition of Slavery and the Social Purity and Temperance movements. Women, at that time, began to realize that in order to transform societal ills they would need to develop their own organizations. The original campaign included a range of issues including the guardianship of infants, property rights, divorce, access to higher education, and equal pay. The early movement would become best known for gaining the right of women to vote in 1920.

Later, during World War II, women began to enter the workforce out of necessity. In doing so, it challenged the stereotype of the traditional stay-at-home mother who was supported by her husband, the sole breadwinner. Then, in the 1960s and 1970s, the women's movement took a more radical turn with the onset of the pill, which initiated the sexual revolution. The pill allowed many women to believe they could have sex whenever they wanted, with whomever they wanted, with no strings attached. In those instances where the pill didn't work, feminists demanded the right to an abortion.

The woman most often referred to as the founder of the radical women's liberation movement was Betty Friedan. In 1963, she authored *The Feminine Mystique*, a book that stated that society puts pressures on women to be housewives and discourages them from seeking a career. In 1966, she founded the National Organization for Women (NOW).

Soon after, Gloria Steinem entered the picture. She, along with Betty Friedan and other women, published the first issue of *Ms.* magazine in 1971 and launched it as a monthly magazine in 1972. Gloria Steinem is known as a primary influence in the sexual revolution of the late 1960s and early 1970s. She discouraged the institution of marriage and once said, "A woman needs a man like a fish needs a bicycle." She later said, "I don't think marriage has a good name. . . . Legally speaking, it was designed for a person and a half. You became a semi-non-person when you got married."[5] While few women were unwilling to shed the institution of marriage at the suggestion of Ms. Steinem, many were influenced to shuck the idea of waiting until marriage to have sex.

Ironically, in 2000, Gloria Steinem wed at the age of sixty-six. Apparently, she became a fish in need of a bicycle. For someone who influenced countless women with her radical views concerning women's rights, she failed in the end to adhere to her own view against marriage. I believe someone like that is properly called a hypocrite. If she couldn't follow through with her own views, why should other women do so?

If Gloria Steinem proved to be an unreliable representative of a movement that influenced masses of women, what about Betty Friedan? In *Betty Friedan, Her Life*, a biography written by Judith Hennessee, the author finds it difficult to reconcile Betty Friedan, the visionary, with Betty Friedan, the woman. It turns out that the "great liberator of women" was ill tempered, selfish, ego-driven, arrogant, and altogether disagreeable. Perhaps most shocking is the fact that Friedan is commonly known as "the feminist who didn't like women!"[6]

How sad that so many women have been led astray by a movement that was led and represented by these two women. They made up the rules as they went along, and when it became convenient or helpful to suit their own personal preferences and agendas, they ignored or changed their rules. Unfortunately, by the time their character flaws were exposed, it was too late. The radical women's movement had gained wings of its own and taken flight.

The words of the apostle Paul ring true of these women in 1 Corinthians 3:18–19: "Do not deceive yourselves. If any one of you thinks he is wise by the standards of this age, he should become a 'fool' so that he may become wise. For the wisdom of this world is foolishness in God's sight. As it is written: 'He catches the wise in their craftiness.'"

So why the history lesson? If we are to understand when the assault on biblical manhood occurred, we must trace it back to its origins—a time when gender roles began to be blurred and a few loud-mouthed, bitter women declared men as the enemy. It is my belief that the sexual revolution, which evolved out of the radical women's liberation movement, is to blame for many of the negative influences facing our sons (and daughters) today. While an objective Christian would have to admit to some merit of the women's movement, such as its justified campaign for equal pay for equal work, overall it has had a devastating impact on both women and men in our society. Because of its campaigns for sexual freedom, abortion on demand, self-empowerment, and antimarriage agendas, we are now reaping the consequences.

While the radical women's liberation movement, led primarily by Friedan and Steinem, seems to have died down, a new and revised version of the women's movement has evolved. Waiting in the wings to take the place of the radical women's liberation movement is what is commonly referred to as "revised feminist ideology." Its message is peddled through television, movies, magazines, music, and other media outlets. It is virtually inescapable.

From Burning Bras to Push-Up Bras

What is "revised feminist ideology"? It is an offshoot of the radical women's liberation movement, minus the extremes. It is pro-career and antagonistic to stay-at-home mothers. It is sexual freedom with no strings attached. It is self-empowerment and independence. It tells girls and women to set their own rules and do whatever feels good because it's all about *them*. In general, it is a message that tells girls and women, "You can have it all!"

The main problem with revised feminist ideology is that it blatantly contradicts itself. Let me explain. One of its major tenets is that women should be independent (i.e., not be dependent on men). Another of its major tenets is that women have the right to sexual freedom. This compares to the messages sent by the radical women's movement, but it has a caveat. The revised tenet sends a message to women that, in short, says: "You can have sex with whomever you want, whenever you want, with no strings attached, but in order to get the man that will enable you to exercise your *freedom*, you must dress scantily and practice shallow 'snag-a-man' magazine tactics." How ironic that the very movement that, on the one hand, preaches women's independence from men, on the other hand encourages women to be dependent on men so they can exercise their sexual freedom! (Of course, you don't hear many guys complaining.)

Compare these "guy magnet" tips to some of my vintage *Seventeen* magazines. In the older *Seventeen* magazines, there were a few ads and articles that gave the reader tips on how to get a guy's attention but centered on products such as hand lotion, scented soap, or perfume. One of my all-time favorite snag-a-man articles had the title, "Make Him a Pie" and pictured four smiling all-American boys holding a fresh-baked pie, no doubt hand delivered from their flock of admirers. Another *Seventeen* magazine from 1960 had an ad that said, "Beats Going Out! A Chef Boy-Ar-Dee pizza convinces boys there's no place like home as no store-bought pizza can." Yet another ad said, "Good date idea . . . Feed him delicious Date Corn Bread—and he can easily see how nice you are!" (I must remember to share that one with my daughter.) The girls in these ads opted for an apron to lure their man rather than cleavage-baring blouses and thong underwear. The ads clearly were based on the old adage that "the way to a man's heart is through his stomach." Call me old-fashioned, but I'd much prefer that the girls bidding for my son's attention do so by flaunting their baked goods rather than their physical goods. Today girls are told that in order to attract the opposite sex, they must flirt, dress provocatively, make the first move, and cultivate their sensuality.

We have the women's liberation movement to thank for the fact that few men open doors for women and surrender their seats to women. Women have been taught that they are far too independent for that. For heaven's sakes, we wouldn't want men to *respect* us, now, would we? Besides, why bother with that kind of respect when women can get respect for so much more—like plunging necklines, bare midriffs, and painted on jeans. Now that's progress! In times long past, men had to pay a cover charge to see women dressed like that. I must remember to pen a thank-you note to Ms. Friedan and Ms. Steinem for spearheading a movement that has redefined *respect* when it comes to the opposite sex.

Girl Power Run Amuck

By now you have probably heard of "girl power," which is basically the juvenile version of revised feminist ideology. It is peddled through the popular media outlets from cartoons (think Kim Possible, the kung fu-fighting cheerleader who saves the world with her goofy and often clueless cohort by her side, Ron Stoppable) to the teen fashion magazines such as *Cosmo's* and *Elle's* little sister spin-offs, *Cosmogirl* and *Elle Girl*. Same biased "girl power" agenda as in the big-girl magazines, just not as many big words.

Let me give you an absurd, even laughable, example of a "girl power" message that landed in my in-box. It was from the popular teen fashion magazine, *Cosmogirl* (the teen version of *Cosmopolitan*). The magazine was promoting a campaign directed at teen girls, called "Girls on Top." In an online teaser ad used to lure girls to participate, here is what I read:

Our bet? In the year 2024, one CosmoGIRL! reader will become president of the United States. The rest of

you will be CEOs, executives, and leaders. Consider this your power road map.

What's your dream? Do you want to make a million dollars by the time you're 25? You'll come home each night to your mansion and kiss your foxy husband and adorable kids hello before you rush to pack for your business trip. And hey, do they want to come with you? Why not? You're the boss! Or maybe you want to be the biggest boss of all. As in world leader. As in president of the United States. No, *CosmoGIRL*—this is no fantasy. Welcome to your reality . . .[7]

Hmmm, I couldn't help but notice they didn't include the possibility that some girls may want to be *mothers*. And puhleese, a million dollars, mansion, and a foxy husband all by the age of twenty-five? Now, that's realistic. Heaven help us all if a Cosmogirl becomes president of the United States. Time to pack up and move to Canada!

It is clear that the barometer to "having it all" is achievement in the workplace. Unfortunately, this "you can have it all" message has encouraged many women to postpone marriage and/or having children in order first to establish themselves in their careers. Does that provide satisfaction to women? A book by Sylvia Ann Hewlett entitled *Creating a Life: Professional Woman and the Quest for Children*, reveals that many professional women who have succumbed to this message and poured themselves into building their careers now feel ripped off and betrayed as they find themselves in their late thirties and early forties unable to have children. The research, published in *Time* magazine, found that more than half of the thirty-five-year-old female professionals surveyed and 42 percent of forty-year-olds were childless. Ms. Hewlett told *Time* magazine that women are "shocked, devastated and angry."[8]

Wait a minute. Am I mistaken, or weren't these major goals of the women's movement? Climb the career ladder. Check.

Bypass marriage. Check. Bypass children. Check. Don't look down until you get to the top. Check. Look out for number one. Check. So what is the problem? These women "have it all" according to the world, right? Success, power, prestige, wealth, nice car, nice house, a closet full of designer clothes and shoes—what more could a modern woman want? Perhaps the very things she gave up to reach these goals.

> They soon forgot His works;
> They did not wait for His counsel,
> But lusted exceedingly in the wilderness,
> And tested God in the desert.
> And He gave them their request,
> But sent leanness into their soul.
> (Ps. 106:13–15 NKJV)

The Message to Boys: Girls Rule and Boys Drool

During a flight layover in Los Angeles on my way home from a speaking engagement, I stumbled upon some items in a boutique that further illustrate the pervasive influence of a girl-power movement gone awry. T-shirts, pencil bags, purses, key chains, and other novelty items geared to preteen and teen girls boldly emblazoned with slogans such as "Boys lie—make them cry," "Boys are stupid; throw rocks at them," and "The stupid factory—where boys are made." The T-shirt that encouraged girls to "throw rocks" at boys showed a stick-figure boy with a bewildered look on his face as rocks sailed straight for his head. Or what about another shirt sporting the slogan, "Boys are goobers—drop anvils on their heads," where the same bewildered stick-figure boy is looking up at an anvil as it approaches his head. Hmmm. Am I missing something here? Is this supposed to be funny? There were plenty of customers browsing through the shirts that day who certainly thought so.

Intrigued at the thought that a company would profit from hate messages geared at our boys, I went to the Web site of the vendor, David and Goliath, Inc. Interesting company name, especially given the fact that David was remembered for being "a man after God's own heart," not to mention the ultimate warrior. It seems blasphemous to couple his good name with a company that produces "stupid boy" slogans. One feature on the site is for girls and women to "send us a stupid boy story." The directions say, "Know any boys? They are stupid! Tell us about that dumb boyfriend, stupid boy at school or gross brother so everyone can see how stupid they really are."[9] It goes on to say that stories submitted may be used in a future catalog or on the company Web site. Creator Todd Goldman defended his antiboy slogans as just a joke. One that gleaned his company $100 million in sales, I might add. Apparently I'm not the only one that sees little to laugh at when it comes to Goldman's "joke." Author Bernard Goldberg released a book, *100 People Who Are Screwing Up America*, and Mr. Goldman ranked number ninety-seven on the list.

Unfortunately, this is not an isolated case of boy bashing. Other vendors have jumped on the bandwagon and cranked out shirts and novelty items with similar slogans such as "I make boys cry," and "Boys are useless, dump them." Now stop for a minute and imagine what would happen if one of these vendors created a shirt sporting the message, "Girls are psycho. Put them in straitjackets." Add a female stick figure with blonde pigtails wrapped tightly in a straitjacket and voilá, you have a product for the guys, right? Wrong. Do you think for a minute that a boy would be allowed to wear such a shirt to school? No way! He'd be sent to the office, and his parents would be notified of his public display of hate rhetoric. Of course, this would never happen because there isn't a retailer out there who would run the risk of carrying such a line of antigirl products. So this begs the question: Why, then, do we shrug off similar hate messages targeted at our boys as "funny"?

Studies are bearing out results that prove it's tough to be a boy in today's world. These results show that more boys than girls are falling behind academically in subjects like math and language skills.[10] More boys than girls are suspended from school, are held back a grade, or drop out of high school.[11] Boys are three times more likely to attend special education classes and four times more likely to receive a diagnosis of ADHD.[12] Could it be that the majority of our time and resources has been devoted to playing catch-up with our girls at the expense of neglecting our boys? Was this the goal—to see our girls jump ahead and leave the boys in their dust? Shouldn't the goal be the equal advancement of both boys and girls?

Most of us have grown calloused to the "males are wimps" message. It is so pervasive that it often goes unnoticed. I recently mentioned to a friend that one of my favorite shows is *Everybody Loves Raymond*, and my friend asked me if it bothered me that much of the humor is at the expense of Raymond being an idiot. It started me thinking that this is more than common in sitcoms from *Home Improvement* to *The King of Queens*. It is prevalent in commercials where the husband or dad character is often displayed as a clueless idiot. Take some of the SUV commercials, for example, where the wife has to leave the trash can behind the car so the rear navigation system will remind clueless hubby to set it on the curb. Or the one where she picks stranded hubby up on the roadside and converts the back into open cargo within seconds to store his bike. Not a word is exchanged, but the message is clear: This is way too complicated for a male to handle—thank goodness, a female is nearby to help.

And we wonder where all the "real" men have gone. The culture has, for the most part, succeeded in wimpifying our men; yet at the same time, we complain about the lack of real men in our society. No one seems to know what a real man is anymore. Is it any wonder our young men are confused? Many Christians are unfamiliar with the foundations of biblical manhood due to the lack of influential and godly role models. Our culture stepped in and redefined manhood while many of us stood on the sidelines and shrugged it off as no big deal. But be not mistaken. It is a huge deal. Unless we go back to the basics of what constitutes a real man and raise our boys accordingly, they will, by default, be molded by a culture that does not produce real men.

Pink Is the New Navy Blue

Perhaps even worse than the "girls are better" message doled out by the girl power forces, is the message that boys should be more like girls. What can be said about a culture that glamorizes homosexuality as chic? Take, for example, the show *Queer Eye for the Straight Guy*. The show's Web site describes their intended mission as "five gay men transform a style-deficient and culture-deprived straight man from drab to fab." Ick.

This and many other influences have led to the new hybrid male—meet the ever-so-urban "metrosexual." While *metrosexual* is a slang term and can't be found in a standard dictionary, the consensus is that it constitutes a heterosexual male who spends inordinate amounts of time on fashion and primping. Some slang definitions go as far as to say it is a heterosexual male with homosexual tendencies. Think boy bands here.

It is important that we distinguish between guys who have more of an artsy urban taste for fashion and those who prioritize vanity with an effeminate flair. I know plenty of strong Christian young men who are attentive to fashion and grooming, and they are not metrosexuals.

I recently read a laugh-out-loud article by Townhall.com columnist Doug Giles. The article was entitled "Metrosexual or Medieval?" and referred to a *Washington Times* report that women are beginning to complain about the shortage of real men. Doug eloquently sums up the article's premise by saying that "American women are pig sick of the oversold and dandy metrosexual male imago." He goes on to say, "American lasses are righteously refusing the low yield, reflexively irate fops Hollywood has tried to cram down our culture's collective throat. The girls have spoken and have said, No thanks, to the eyebrow-tweaked man."[13] Amen, brother Doug! He even gives a self-quiz for men to determine if they are candidates for the metrosexual label. Of course it is meant to be tongue-in-cheek, but it offers a more detailed definition of what this slang term means. He includes such defining factors as:

- You use more than three words when ordering your Starbucks.
- You buy your shampoo at a salon instead of the grocery store.
- You put on cologne to go to the gym.
- You take more than two minutes to fix your hair.
- You think you have a feminine side to get in touch with.[14]

The "metro" trend was cultivated by media forces that glamorize homosexuality as chic and trendy. I hope it will be a passing phase, and our men will get back to the business of being men. We are in desperate need of men who will step up to the plate and lead their families and defend their country both here and abroad. Call it a hunch, but I'm not sure the military would have much tolerance for the "metro-man." If he holds up the line while primping in front of the bathroom mirror at base camp or attempts to trade in his metal canteen for bottled water, I'm betting that it won't be pretty. I'm fairly certain the base camp barber doesn't do highlights.

Boys Will Be Boys . . . Indefinitely?

I opened this chapter with a description of actual ads that can be found in vintage *Seventeen* magazines from the 1940s–1960s. The expectation of marriage was a major theme throughout the magazines. The average age for marriage in 1950 for males was twenty-two, and the average age for females was twenty,[15] so this more than explains the plethora of product placement ads for engagement rings, sterling silver flatware, and Lane hope chests. The pro-marriage emphasis stayed strong throughout the 1950s and even into the 1960s. As the sexual revolution and the women's movement began to gather momentum in the 1960s and 1970s, the ads began to dwindle. Perhaps the greatest assault to the foundation of biblical manhood is that young men today are not encouraged to grow up.

In a fabulous column entitled, "What If There Are No Grown-ups?" Albert Mohler makes the point that

> in days gone by, children learned how to be adults by living, working, and playing at the parents' side. The onset of age twelve or thirteen meant that time was running out on childhood. Traditional ceremonies like the Jewish *Bar Mitzvah* announced that adulthood was dawning. This point would be clearly understood by the young boy undergoing the *Bar Mitzvah*. "By the time his body was fully formed, he would be expected to do a full day's work. He could expect to enter the ranks of full-fledged grownups soon after and marry in his late teens. Childhood was a swift passageway to adulthood, and adulthood was a much-desired state of authority and respect."[16]

By 1980, the average age for men marrying for the first time had jumped to twenty-four and the average age for women jumped to twenty-two.[17] In 2000, the average age for men marrying was at 26.8, the oldest age in the nation's history, and the average age for women marrying was 25.1.[18] At first glance the results may not indicate a cause for concern, but one cannot help but wonder where it will stop. David Popenoe, a Rutgers sociology professor and codirector of the National Marriage Project, stated that "if this trend of men waiting to marry continues, it is likely to clash with the timing of marriage and childbearing for the many young women who hope to marry and bear children before they begin to face problems associated with declining fertility."[19]

So what does all this really mean and, more important, how does it impact our sons? For starters, there are few pressures in place for men to wed and eventually start a family. Think about it. Why would men rush into marriage if they can postpone responsibility and opt instead to hookup or shack up with one or more of the many women who are willing to practice their sexual freedom? But is this what women really want? I don't think so. A study sponsored by the Independent Women's Forum called "Hooking Up, Hanging Out, and Hoping for Mr. Right" further proved that our sexually promiscuous culture is not without heavy emotional consequences. The study found an alarming trend of young people hooking up for casual sex without any promise of commitment or long-term relationships. The report was based on surveys of college women who all but confirmed that traditional dating is a thing of the past.

The independence and empowerment promised to women by the sexual revolution as a result of no-commitment hook ups has left young women feeling anything but empowered. In fact, 61 percent of survey respondents said that a hookup makes them feel "desirable" but also "awkward." Additionally, 83 percent of respondents agreed that "being married is a very important goal for me."[20] The survey results showed that in spite of sexual freedom, most women are incapable of viewing sex as a casual encounter absent of emotional consequences. One Princeton grad summed it up this way: "The whole thing is a very male-dominated scene. Hooking up lets men get physical pleasure without any emotional connection, but for the women it's hard to separate the physical from the emotional. Women want the call the next day."[21]

In spite of the fact that college women in the study above admitted that marriage was an important goal for them, many will still not get their wish unless they are willing to shack up first. No doubt the sexual revolution and its encouragement for hooking up and cohabitation offer men many of the benefits they seek from marriage without the obligations and commitment. Between 1960 and 2000, the number of unmarried couples in America increased by over 1,000 percent.[22] About ten million people are living together with a partner outside of marriage, which adds up to about 8 percent of the coupled households in America.[23] About 44 percent of single men, aged twenty to twenty-nine, agree with the statement that they would only marry someone if she agreed to live together first.[24] Seventy percent of teens believe that a couple living together outside of marriage is acceptable. Think our Christian teens are the exceptions? The same study found that 50 percent of churchgoing teens find it acceptable.[25] I wonder if the men who are giving cohabitation a big thumbs-up are aware that studies have shown that couples who live together before marriage are twice as likely to divorce as those who do not.

Why, then, are so many men bent on cohabitation? One of the top ten reasons men cited in a study conducted by The National Marriage Project was—get ready for this one—"the convenience of having a regular sex partner."[26] Another reason men cited for living with a woman was that it reduced the risks of sex with strangers.[27] My grandmother's words of wisdom ring in my ears: "Why buy the cow if you can get the milk for free?" In summary, the study concludes, "In the past, of course, men might drag their feet about getting hitched, but there were pressures to wed. Marriage was associated with growing up and taking on male adult roles and responsibilities. Parents expected sons to leave and set up their own household. Now the pressures to wed are mild to nonexistent. Boys can remain boys indefinitely."[28] And recent survey results indicate that most "boys" plan to live up to the cliché.

In a thought-provoking essay addressing the problem of stunted maturity among men, author Frederica Mathewes-Green states that

God designed our bodies to desire to mate much earlier, and through most of history cultures have accom-
modated that desire by enabling people to wed by their
late teens or early twenties. People would postpone
marriage until their late twenties only in cases of eco-
nomic disaster or famine—times when people had to
save up in order to marry.[29]

And what about those who encourage the delay of marriage as
a preventative measure to avoiding divorce? Mathewes-Green
notes that "fifty years ago, when the average bride was twenty,
the divorce rate was half what it is now, because the culture
encouraged and sustained marriage."[30]

The negative attitudes about marriage perpetuated by the
women's movement and the sexual revolution have produced
devastating fallout. Here is a summary of the damage:

- The average American spends most of his or her life
  unmarried.[31]
- Dating is all but obsolete and has been replaced by
  casual hooking-up.[32]
- There is an increase in "serial cohabitation," or living
  with one partner for a time, then moving on to another.[33]
- The majority of couples marrying today have lived
  together first.[34]
- Houses headed by unmarried partners (single fathers,
  single mothers, and gay couples) increased significantly,
  while houses headed by a married couple, for the first
  time ever, fell to below 25 percent of all households.[35]
- Almost six in ten marriages will end in divorce.[36]
- Born-again Christians are just as likely to have been
  divorced as are nonborn-again adults. Over 90 percent
  of such born-again Christians experienced their divorce
  after becoming born again.[37]

- Forty percent of children will go to bed each night without having a biological father living in their home to tuck them in.[38]
- Almost half of all children will spend part of their years living in a single-parent home.[39]
- About two-fifths of children are expected to live in a cohabitating household at some point.[40]
- A third of all births are to unmarried women. Compare this to 3.8 percent in 1940.[41]

You may be wondering: *Why the big deal? What do the current attitudes regarding marriage have to do with biblical manhood?* Without delving into the obvious factor that marriage is God's plan for procreation, it represents much more. Throughout Scripture, God compares the union of marriage to the union of Christ and his bride (the church.) In a nutshell, God loves marriage and created it not only for the enjoyment of his people but also to bring glory and honor to him. God hates cohabitation. God hates hooking up. God hates it when children are born out of wedlock. God hates divorce. God is pro-family and, therefore, God is pro-marriage. God will call some to remain single, and this in no way minimizes their worth and value in God's eyes, but the truth is, God will call most to marry. When the union of marriage is minimized, mocked, or emulated by cohabitation or homosexual unions, it will alter the gender roles and responsibilities that God intended for men (and women). We are seeing in our society today an identity crisis when it comes to defining gender roles.

In spite of the negative rap that marriage has been given over the last several decades, a 2004 study of one thousand heterosexual men (both married and unmarried) by the National Marriage Project documented the following pro-marriage attitudes among men:

- Ninety-four percent of married men say that they are happier being married than being single.

- Seventy-three percent of married men say their sex lives are better since getting married.
- Only 36 percent of unmarried men agree, "Single men have better sex lives than married men."
- Sixty-eight percent say marriage has helped them become more financially stable.[42]

I find it ironic that in spite of the campaign to malign the union of marriage and diminish its importance, marriage continues to be a goal among men and women in the quest for fulfillment and happiness. Could it be that independence, aloneness, hooking up, shacking up, and other prescriptions for "happiness" peddled by the culture, in the end, leave us empty? God wired us for intimacy, first and foremost with him. But let us remember that Adam was once a single man with the world at his fingertips. He had everything a single man could want, including a thriving relationship with Almighty God. Yet something was still missing. God determined that "it is not good for the man to be alone" (Gen. 2:18). God created woman to reduce man's aloneness and give him someone with whom to share the joys and sorrows of life. Unfortunately, our culture has forgotten, or has chosen to ignore, the origins of marriage as dictated by a Holy God.

The good news is that the above-mentioned study also found that married and unmarried men from traditional family and religious backgrounds have more positive attitudes toward women, children, and marriage.[43] This offers proof that a mom's faithfulness to pass down positive attitudes about marriage and family to her sons (and daughters) can and does influence their attitudes about marriage and family. Marriage will survive. The key question is whether the biblical model for marriage will *thrive*.

Our culture has made a mess of manhood. It has blurred gender lines, maligned masculinity, and mocked the institution of marriage. The next chapter will offer a practical guide to aid mothers in passing down the formula for a virtuous wife. Finally, the last chapter will present a basic blueprint for raising a "real man." I say "basic" because entire books could be written on the topic of biblical manhood. For some it will serve as an encouragement that you are on the right track as you are raising your son. For others it will serve as a wake-up call that you have been using the wrong blueprint or no blueprint at all.

CHAPTER 12

Passing Down the Formula for a Virtuous Wife

In the introduction, I mentioned that writing this book has been a bittersweet experience because my older son will graduate from high school several months after this book releases. At the time of this writing, he is days shy of entering his senior year. This manuscript is due to my publisher in just two short weeks. I now know that the timing in all of this is no accident. I have written these words through the lens of a mother who is about to launch her boy into real life. And, yes, I am scared out of my wits. I have labored over every chapter and second-guessed my own parenting—sometimes silently asking, *Did I do this? Did he get it? Will it be enough?* I cannot begin to tell you the sense of urgency I feel at this moment.

I was struck with the overwhelming sense of urgency and the endless series of "what ifs" playing through my mind. *What if he dates girls in college who are not strong Christians? Or even worse, what if she is not a Christian at all? What if he fails to recognize huge character flaws along the way that could doom a marriage should it come to that? What if he chooses a bride based on his own preference rather than God's will?*

He will likely marry, so with this thought at the forefront of my mind and the clock ticking in the background, I have written this chapter for myself—as a purging of sorts. But I have also written it for my son. I plan to take the time in the final months before he leaves for college to go over this chapter with him. I have taught him these truths over the years in bits and pieces, here and there. But I'm not sure I have taken the time to sit down with him formally and talk about God's standards for a virtuous woman. When it comes time to pack his belongings and send him on his way, this chapter will follow him. Whether he will read it and choose to follow its wisdom will, in the end, be up to him. In the meantime, he has my vote of confidence.

Regardless of your son's age, this chapter is a must-read. Obviously, the truths contained herein will bear the greatest results when put into practice in the years leading up to your son's senior year. With that said, let's look to God's Word for the best wisdom available when it comes to what sort of qualities our sons should look for when choosing a life mate.

The "Virtuous" Checklist

When it comes to offering our sons advice regarding a future mate, there is no better guide than Proverbs 31. It is speculated that King Lemuel wrote the passage as he reflected on his mother's teaching regarding the type of wife he should seek (which, if you ask me, gives us the same right!). It is thought that the poem did not originate with King Lemuel's mother but was actually a freestanding poem that had been passed down for many generations for the purpose of aiding men in identifying an ideal wife as well as giving women a formula for becoming the ideal wife. The twenty-two verses are in an acrostic format with each verse beginning with consecutive letters of the Hebrew alphabet to aid in easy memorization. While, at first glance, the Proverbs 31 woman may appear to be an outdated fixture of the past; her character qualities stand the test of time. The passage is just as meaningful today as it was when it was originally written. Be reminded, "All Scripture is God-breathed and is useful for teaching, rebuking, correcting and training in righteousness" (2 Tim. 3:16).

I wonder how many divorces could have been avoided if the groom had used Proverbs 31 as a guideline for choosing his future mate. Our sons should be taught the importance of Proverbs 31 for recognizing the qualities of a noble wife. It should be noted that there is speculation that the passage is not a description of one actual woman but rather a compilation of positive qualities that many different women might have. It would be unreasonable to expect any young lady to display 100 percent of the qualities listed in the passage, especially considering the fact that most of us are still in pursuit of these qualities and will be until we breathe our last breath. That having being said, below you will find a "virtuous woman" checklist. Come graduation day, make sure your son is well versed in the passage and doesn't leave home without it! I have included key questions for your son, should he be open to measuring potential brides against God's standards for a virtuous woman. (Also note, if you have daughters, this is a great chapter to go with them to ensure they are in the process of becoming virtuous women.)

A wife of noble character who can find?
She is worth far more than rubies. (Prov. 31:10)

Our sons should be made aware of how rare this type of woman is and should be encouraged to hold out for the best . . . God's best. If they find her, they have found a treasure. She is not like most other girls (including Christian girls!) who have conformed themselves to the culture.

Key questions for your son: Would this young lady be described by others with words like "virtuous," "moral," and "noble"? Even if she has a past, would these words describe who she is today?

Her husband has full confidence in her and lacks nothing
of value. She brings him good, not harm, all the days of
her life. (Prov. 31:11–12)

This woman is every man's dream come true. She is not a whiner, nor does she bite back with attitude and sarcasm. I am reminded of Proverbs 27:15, "A quarrelsome wife is like a constant dripping on a rainy day." We all know women like this who make life miserable for all in their household. A virtuous woman is not a nagger; she puts the needs of her husband before her own.

Key questions for your son: Does this young lady have a temper? Is she in the habit of complaining and nagging? Does she easily hold grudges and struggle to forgive others?

> *She selects wool and flax and*
> *works with eager hands.*
> *She is like the merchant ships,*
> *bringing her food from afar.*
> *She gets up while it is still dark; she provides food for her*
> *family and portions for her servant girls.*
> *She considers a field and buys it; out of her earnings she*
> *plants a vineyard.*
> *She sets about her work vigorously;*
> *her arms are strong for her tasks.*
> *She sees that her trading is profitable,*
> *and her lamp does not go out at night.*
> *In her hand she holds the distaff and*
> *grasps the spindle with her fingers. . . .*
> *She makes linen garments and sells them, and supplies the*
> *merchants with sashes.*
> *(Prov. 31:13–19, 24)*

This woman is no slacker. She is hardworking and devoted to her work. She is assertive and decisive, and her confidence shines through in all she does. She is strong, yet it does not diminish her femininity.

Key questions for your son: Does this young lady have a princess attitude and expect others to serve her? Is she lazy and demotivated in life, or is she devoted to the task at hand and committed to hard work?

> *She opens her arms to the poor and extends her hands to the needy. (Prov. 31:20)*

This woman is kind and compassionate. She is attentive to the needs of those less fortunate. She is not so self-absorbed that she turns a blind eye to suffering.

Key questions for your son: What is her attitude about mission work? Has she been involved in a mission trip or project that helps those who are less fortunate? Or is she focused on her own needs?

> *When it snows, she has no fear for her household; for all of them are clothed in scarlet.*
> *She makes coverings for her bed; she is clothed in fine linen and purple . . .*
> *She watches over the affairs of her household and does not eat the bread of idleness.*
> *(Prov. 31:21–22, 27)*

This woman takes seriously her role as manager of the home. "Lazy" would never be a word used to describe her. She is an astute manager and proficient at delegation.

Key questions for your son: What sort of manager is the young lady in question? Can she delegate, work efficiently, and see a project through to completion? What is her attitude in regard to someday managing a home? What role will she play? Does this line up with what you had in mind?

> *Her husband is respected at the city gate, where he takes his seat among the elders of the land.*
> *(Prov. 31:23)*

This speaks directly to the character of our sons and begs the question of whether they are worthy of such a rare treasure of a virtuous woman.

Key questions for your son: Are you respected by others? Are you a leader (the right kind) among your peers? Do your knowledge and wisdom come from the world, or are they gleaned from time spent in God's Word?

> *She is clothed with strength and dignity;*
> *she can laugh at the days to come. (Prov. 31:25)*

This woman is poised and holds her head high. She has the rare quality of exhibiting a confident trust in God for the future.

Key questions for your son: Has this young lady learned the art of leaning on God when times are uncertain? Or does she busy herself trying to manipulate and fix things to produce a particular outcome? Does she pray and give matters over to God?

> *She speaks with wisdom, and faithful*
> *instruction is on her tongue. (Prov. 31:26)*

This woman does not waste her words on foolish matters. Her wisdom is sought after and her words are soothing. She does not involve herself in gossip or pettiness. Such things are beneath her.

Key questions for your son: Is this young lady a busybody who thrives on the latest gossip? Does she have her hands in everything, including matters that are not her own?

> *Her children arise and call her blessed;*
> *her husband also, and he praises her: "Many women do*
> *noble things, but you surpass them all." (Prov. 31:28–29)*

This woman has earned the respect of her husband and children. They recognize that she is a rare find and feel sincerely blessed.

Key questions for your son: Is this the type of girl others think is a catch? Not based on her appearance but, rather, on her devotion to family and primarily her God. Would others label her "high maintenance"? Can you honestly say that she "surpasses them all"?

> *Charm is deceptive, and beauty is fleeting; but a woman*
> *who fears the* LORD *is to be praised.*
> *(Prov. 31:30)*

This woman does not allow herself to be influenced by the world's obsession with beauty. She recognizes that true beauty comes from the heart. Her most precious quality is the awe and reverence she has for her God. She loves Jesus Christ above all else—he is her *everything*.

Key questions for your son: Is this young lady obsessed with her reflection in the mirror? Do issues of vanity consume her? Has she found the balance between taking pride in her appearance but not emphasizing it as more important than inner beauty? Is she more in awe of God than herself . . . and you?

> *Give her the reward she has earned, and let her works*
> *bring her praise at the city gate. (Prov. 31:31)*

What mother would not want her son to marry such a woman, who at the end of her life will receive the praises of heaven? As mothers, we should commit ourselves to pray fervently for our sons: first, to be worthy of such a woman and, second, to refuse to compromise for anything less.

Key questions for your son: Would this young lady be the type to do the sort of good deeds that would yield her praises at the city gate? Is she known (already) for her devotion to God?

Actions Speak Louder than Words

If you were to sum up the heart of the Proverbs 31 woman with one quality, it would be her ability to fear the Lord. If we desire our sons to recognize this critical quality in a potential bride, we must model it in our own lives. It is more likely to make an impact on our sons if it is caught in addition to being taught. In my book *The Virtuous Woman: Shattering the Superwoman Myth*, which is an overview of Proverbs 31, I said this:

> The virtuous woman's ability to fear God was at the very core of her being. Without it, one could argue that it would be impossible to develop the other attributes spoken of in the passage.

In fact, Psalm 111:10 and Proverbs 9:10 clearly say that "the fear of the LORD is the beginning of wisdom."

Of what use is wisdom unless it is rooted in a reverent fear of the Lord? The virtuous woman of Proverbs 31 was not interested in the brand of wisdom that comes from human knowledge. She sought the same godly wisdom that Job, David, and Solomon sought. Why settle for wisdom that is limited by our own human thinking when we can have access to God's way of thinking? Our sons will meet many young ladies who, for all practical purposes, appear to be "good wife" material; but if they lack this one critical quality of fearing the Lord, it is of no avail. A woman who does not fear the Lord will make choices and determine her life course based on human instinct or, worse, based on "what feels right." On the contrary, a woman who fears the Lord will make choices and consider her steps by running them through the filter of God's will. What have you modeled to your son when it comes to fearing the Lord? It's a tough question, but it needs to be asked. So rare is this woman who fears the Lord that unless your son has seen such a woman in action, he may not know she even exists. As Christians, we belabor the point that our children need to marry fellow Christians, but why not take it a step further. It is possible to be a Christian and exhibit little fear of the Lord. I dare say this is where most believers fall today.

If you truly desire for your son not just to marry a Christian young lady but to marry a Christian young lady who fears the Lord, it will start with you. Does he hear you speak of God often? Does he see you spending time in God's Word? Does he hear you pouring out your heart to God in prayer? Does he know that you find the answers to life's questions from God through his Word and prayer? Does he see a mother who is devoted to her local church? Does he know that God is the source of your happiness and strength? Does he hear you offering thanks to your God? Since the time my children were young, they have heard me voice my gratitude to God for everything from a sunny day to needed rain to quench the earth. They have heard me on many occasions say, "Let me pray about that." They have seen me moved to tears over lyrics from worship choruses that remind me of God's forgiveness. I have always wanted them to know without a shadow of a doubt that I am desperately dependent on God. Without him I am a mess. It is critical to remember that unless our sons marry young women who fear the Lord, they will marry young women who are messes or will become messes.

If your heart is heavy upon reading this and you feel you have not modeled the example of the Proverbs 31 woman of virtue to your son, do not dismay. If your heart is sincere and your motives are pure, it's not too late to begin today. Don't do it for his sake; do it for your own. "Happy are those who fear the LORD. Yes, happy are those who delight in doing what he commands" (Ps. 112:1 NLT). "The fear of the LORD leads to life: Then one rests content, untouched by trouble" (Prov. 19:23 NIV). "Humility and the fear of the LORD bring wealth and honor and life" (Prov. 22:4 NIV). This is only a taste of the blessings that await a woman who fears the Lord. Begin by praying and asking God to help you as you turn your focus to him on a daily basis. Try to develop the habit of catching yourself throughout the day when you face sudden decisions and run them past God. If you are not part of a local Bible-teaching, Christ-honoring church of caring believers, begin the search for such a church right away.

Finally, if your son is older and has left the nest or is about to do so, sit him down and admit your mistake. Humbly tell him that you failed to be a proper example to him of what a woman who fears the Lord is like. As he sees your humility and the evidence that you fear the Lord, he will be more open to accepting your counsel regarding the characteristics his future bride should have. If the Proverbs 31 passage is overwhelming to you and seems out of reach, I highly recommend you read my book, *The Virtuous Woman*. It approaches the quest to be a virtuous woman with a heavy emphasis on grace and mercy.

A Warning against Picking Your Future Daughter-in-law

Trust me when I say I am writing this one for myself. I am famous for torturing my boys with endless suggestions about impressive qualities I have noticed in certain girls from school or the youth group. Rather than rush up to their rooms to add the girl's name to a list of potential marriage candidates, they usually reply with a sarcastic, "Mom, give it up!" Now, as my older son approaches graduation, the tyranny of the urgent has set in. The reality that he might meet his future bride in college has caused me to spring into gear as my window of opportunity closes.

Let me clarify that I do not think there is anything at all wrong with pointing out noble qualities that certain young ladies possess. In fact, I would argue that we have a responsibility to give our sons guidance when it comes to the girls they date and eventually marry. Let us not forget that in Bible times families were a tight-knit group and parents were attentive to whom their sons spent time with. It would be safe to assume that parents were likely familiar with their son's future spouse and her family of origin. Because we don't have this luxury, we owe it to our sons to offer as much guidance as possible while they are still in the nest and under our influence.

That having been said, I would refrain from being so bold as to mention to your son the names of girls who you feel are qualified to someday take your last name. It is a bit presumptuous to assume that we have a straight line to God when it comes to who our future daughters-in-law should be. Rather, I suggest we should stick to focusing on selling the quality that caught our attention rather than the whole girl. (My experience has been that my son is receptive to hearing about a particular girl's qualities but resistant when I go so far as to play matchmaker.) Our goal should be to take advantage of teachable moments where we can point out to our sons the positive qualities we notice in certain girls. When it comes time for our sons to choose brides, we can hope and pray that they will reflect back on our teachings and counsel, but we should leave it to God to reveal to them whom they should marry.

We need to shed our own mental checklist of what constitutes the perfect bride for our sons. I am ashamed to say that I am guilty of having such a checklist. Some of the qualifiers on my list are such things as: saved themselves for marriage; a like-minded stable Christian family; strong, committed church background; and has completed a minimum of six Beth Moore Bible studies. I was fine with my mental checklist until one day it dawned on me that had my mother-in-law passed off such a list to her son, I would not have made the cut! While there is nothing wrong with expressing concerns to our sons over extremely dysfunctional family backgrounds or sordid pasts, it should be done for the purpose of acknowledging possible hurdles that they would have to overcome should they marry such girls. We need to remember that as long as God is at the center of a marriage relationship, great things are possible. I even know of one young woman who had a not-so-virtuous past, came to Christ in her college years, and went on to start a ministry called "Virtuous Reality" and write books on (of all things) *virtue*.

Be Careful How You Pray!

Last but not least, we should be faithful in praying for our sons' future spouses, should it be in God's will for them to marry. Did you notice the last part to that sentence? We need to be careful not to pass off to our sons an expectation that they will marry. While it might be *our* preference, it may not be God's. The emphasis (not to mention, presumption!) on marriage might imply that it is necessary for fulfillment. Only God can fulfill or complete our sons, whether single or married. Given that, I make it a habit to pray, "Father, I lift up my children's future spouses, should it be in your will for them to marry."

Even if your son is still young, it is never too early to pray for his future spouse (given the caveats above) as well as become familiar with the characteristics in Proverbs 31. Before you know it, you will find yourself with a son who is ready to fly the nest, and you will wonder where in the world the time went. At that point, you will be left to pray that your previously spoken words and counsel will stick. In the meantime, we have our work cut out for us in the here and now, as we raise our sons to be the kind of young men who are worthy of noble and virtuous wives.

CHAPTER 13

Raising Your Boy to Be a Real Man

A friend sent me an article last year that left me feeling rather conflicted. It is from *Men's Health* magazine and is entitled "Babes in Boyland." The blurb reads, "Women are charging out of college, determined to take on the world—with or without a guy at their side, even when the time comes to raise a family. Are men prepared to meet the challenge?"[1]

The author, a modern-day single woman, starts by reflecting back on a trip to Mexico with a girlfriend. They really wanted their boyfriends to join them, but the author says, "They are stuck at home, short on cash—as usual. This happens a lot. Though we're hardly what you'd call fast-trackers . . . we still outearn the men we love, who are talented and smart but, let's say, motivationally challenged, career development-wise."[2] The article presents daunting statistics that reveal more women than men attend college today (fifty-six women for every forty-four men),[3] female college graduates start working sooner than their male counterparts,[4] and job status and security now matter more to young women than to their male peers.[5]

"We're speeding along life's highway, and our men aren't even on the ramp yet. . . . While you're sowing your wild oats, listening to terrible music, and letting the dishes pile up in the sink, we've begun building careers and 401(k)s. We're buying cars, applying for mortgages, and generally behaving like grown-ups."[6]

The author mentions that the key to understanding today's young single woman is what she calls the "catch-35," due to the fact that in the back of every woman's mind is the knowledge that after age thirty-five the chances of having problems with pregnancy or birth increase exponentially. Because of this catch-35, women feel an enormous amount of pressure to make their mark in the workforce before their mid-thirties. "Men face few penalties for postponing marriage," the Rutgers National Marriage Project asserts. "Unlike women over 30, they do not have to worry about a ticking biological clock. Nor do they have to obey a sociological 'clock.'"

In a 2001 nationwide survey of 1,003 men and women ages twenty-one to twenty-nine by Rutgers University, 82 percent agreed that it's unwise for a woman to rely on marriage for financial security.[7] You can hardly blame the young women for taking matters into their own hands, especially considering the disturbing lack of motivation found among many of their male peers. What would our grandparents' generation say about this? Single men of the past prepared for the day when they would get married and provide for their families. Sure, there are two sides to every story, and we must remember that many of our men have been beaten and battered into submission by the antimale forces in our country. But, c'mon! Did they just roll over and die?

And what about the young women who were described in the article above? Are we supposed to be impressed at their independence, portfolios, and stick-to-itiveness when it comes to climbing the career ladder? The author proudly acknowledges that she and many of her female peers are driven by "three unchanging goals: (1) achieving a level of professional accomplishment that will lead to (2) financial independence, allowing us to (3) start a family by the time we're 35—whether or not there's a man around to share it with."[8]

She states that they have a good decade and a half to "work" toward accomplishing their goals before their chances of infertility increase. I found it amazing that she casually speaks of starting a family as if it's something you cross off your to-do list. Has she ever been around any hardworking single moms? Apparently not, or she would not have such a laissez-faire attitude about single parenting. What a sad and pathetic statement, which is reflective of the culture today. Is this really progress? The whole article left me feeling depressed for my own children, not to mention the author.

A Real Man Is a Provider

I picked up a book shortly after reading the above-mentioned article that left me a bit more encouraged. Shaunti Feldhahn's best-selling book *For Women Only* surveyed four hundred men randomly across the country (between the ages of twenty-one and seventy-five) and had them answer two dozen questions about how they think, what they feel, and what they need. As a follow-up to the survey, she surveyed four hundred more men (specifically, churchgoers) with some of the same questions. The two surveys yielded basically the same results, which Feldhahn condensed into seven revelations about the inner lives of men. I found the entire book fascinating and have recommended it to many women. However, one revelation was particularly insightful when it comes to a man's role as provider. The question was worded this way: "Suppose your wife/significant other earned enough to support your family's lifestyle. Would you still feel a compulsion to provide for your family? Seventy-six percent of men said yes, while 21 percent said no."[9]

Interview after interview confirmed this compulsion men feel to provide. Even more astounding is that 71 percent of men surveyed said that the responsibility to provide is *always* or *often* on their mind. The survey indicated that being a provider is at the very core of a man's identity and worth.[10] It did not matter how much his wife/partner earned; it is wired deep within his identity that he is meant to provide for his family. In one interview the man's wife was sitting next to him as he expressed the burden/compulsion he feels to provide for his family. His wife chimed in, "But I've always worked! I've always contributed to the family budget!" to which he gently replied, "You working or not is irrelevant. Not to the family budget—it does ease some of the financial pressure. But it is irrelevant to my *need* to provide."[11]

How do we reconcile the results of the survey above that states that "men want to provide" with the premise of the article that preceded it that "men are unmotivated slackers" (my summation)? If the majority of men feel a compelling need to provide, why, then, are so many dragging out their boyhood years by avoiding the responsibility? An essay that I cited in the last chapter by author Frederica Mathewes-Green may provide part of the answer. She addresses, among many things, this current trend of men who avoid growing up. She believes that parents of the baby boomers have separated childhood and adulthood into two completely different compartments of life. Childhood is marked by innocence, and adulthood is marked by responsibility.[12] She makes a great point. Can it be that we, as parents, are partly to blame for this current trend of prolonged boyhood? Rather than help our children make the transition from childhood to adulthood in their teen years prior to leaving the nest, we have treated the first eighteen years as the official "childhood" period. Once they graduate, we send them out into the world (if you can get them to leave) to make the transition into adulthood alone, in their own timing, and on their own terms. Call it the self-paced journey to manhood, if you will.

What can we, as mothers of sons, learn from this? First, if it is true that being a provider is deeply ingrained within the heart of every man and, further, it is true that not providing makes a man feel less of a man, we must become their cheerleaders when it comes to providing. In spite of the fact that our sons will grow up in a culture where women no longer count on them to provide, we must help our sons realize that God still does. Second, we must be purposeful in helping our sons make the transition into manhood before they leave home. We must clearly verbalize the expectations that come with manhood, and we must show them what is involved in this rite of passage. Finally, we must put our sons to work, literally. It will do little good if action does not follow instruction. "If a man is lazy, the rafters sag; if his hands are idle, the house leaks" (Eccl. 10:18).

My husband has done an outstanding job of helping our sons in their journey to manhood. He has worked hard over the years to teach both Ryan and his younger brother, Hayden, necessary life skills. He has taught them financial responsibility and the importance of saving and tithing a portion of their incomes. Most important, he has modeled a strong work ethic to our boys by being a provider in our home. In addition to modeling a work ethic, he insisted that Ryan work a summer job beginning at the age of sixteen. Every aspect of the process from filling out the application, interviewing for the job, training for the job, showing up on time, keeping track of his schedule, communicating with his employer, setting up a checking account, depositing his paychecks, and managing his own money are critical life skills.

Initially, I wrestled with the thought that our son should forego a summer job and get ahead by taking extra classes over the summer. In the end I agreed that a job would be a far better investment in his future.

His first job was at a locally owned hot dog restaurant. I knew we had made a wise move when I met the owner shortly after he got the job. She told me that her training philosophy for her employees was to train them in every area from cooking, running the cash register, busing tables—and here's the good part—mopping the floors and cleaning the bathrooms! After his first day on the job, Ryan came home near tears, explaining that he had to cut up vegetables for hours, and the job wasn't at all what he had imagined. After a few more days of performing other tedious tasks, he came home and announced that he was quitting. It provided yet another teachable moment for my husband and me to educate him to the fact that there are aspects to every job that are not enjoyable. He stuck with the job for the entire summer, and it ended up being a wonderful experience. The owner told him he was one of the best employees she had ever had and left the door open for future summer employment.

This past summer he worked a full forty hours a week (at the age of seventeen) doing hard, manual labor for a business owner at our church. While many of his friends slept in, went to the lake, or vegged in front of a TV, Ryan mowed lawns in 100-degree heat, moved furniture, mulched cedar trees, cleaned pools, ran errands, and even trapped and disposed of a skunk. (I won't go into details on the methodology, but trust me, he earned his warrior badge that day!)

Thanks to his dad, Ryan has learned the value of hard work. Since they were very young, Keith has always been adamant that our children do chores. He has involved our boys in such chores as changing tires, building decks, cleaning out air-conditioner vents, basic yard work, cutting and bundling tree limbs, and other "manly" chores. While it would be easier for him just to do it himself, he recognizes the value of investing the time to train our sons in preparation for the future.

I realize that there will be many single mothers, or even married women, who do not have husbands who are willing to take on the responsibility of training their sons around the house. If this is your situation, you will carry the burden of this critical responsibility. If your son is young, start by giving him basic chores around the house. As he gets older, involve him in projects where older adult men are present, like keeping up the grounds at the church or helping a male neighbor or relative with building projects. Many of my female friends take care of the lawn work and enjoy household building projects. If you are adept at these things, consider involving your son in the process, especially if he does not have a male role model in the picture to train him. The bottom line is to get your boy to work. If you do not make it a priority, your son will do what comes naturally, which is to sit around and play video games, watch television, and/or sleep halfway through the day. Our lack of commitment to teach our boys the value of hard work can stifle their inner drive to be a provider.

In 1 Timothy 5:8, Paul exhorts men and says, "But if any provide not for his own, and specially for those of his own house, he hath denied the faith, and is worse than an infidel" (KJV). Ouch. Do you remember Adam's sentence in the garden for eating the forbidden fruit?

> And He said to Adam, "Because you listened to your wife's voice and ate from the tree about which I commanded you, 'Do not eat from it': The ground is cursed because of you. You will eat from it by means of painful labor all the days of your life. It will produce thorns and thistles for you, and you will eat the plants of the field. You will eat bread by the sweat of your brow until you return to the ground, since you were taken from it. For you are dust, and you will return to dust." (Gen. 3:17–19 HCSB)

Now stop for a minute and think about it. Do you think it is any coincidence that men today still feel a compulsion to provide for their families? Could it be that the compulsion they feel is because God wired them to "eat bread by the sweat of their brow"? We would be wise to follow Scripture when it comes to encouraging our sons to be future providers as designated by God.

Does this mean that a man is less of a provider if his wife works? Absolutely not. I know plenty of hardworking men whose wives work, and it does not diminish their role as providers. A man could bring home a million dollars annually, but if he is only able to do so by being a workaholic, he is a poor provider for his family. The role of provider is more about an attitude of the heart than the number of digits on a paycheck.

While my work as an author and speaker brings in an income, my husband is still the primary provider in our home. He relishes his role as provider, and I do not envy him the position one bit. Should I ever outearn my husband (not likely, given that I am in the ministry!), my husband will still be the primary provider in our home. Interpret that however you would like, but it is my prayer that my sons will also be recognized as providers in their homes. My husband has modeled to my sons a strong work ethic not just in regard to working a job but also in taking care of odd jobs in and around the house. (He is not too proud to do housework when I have a book deadline looming!) He has also managed our money efficiently and provided a nest egg for our children's college education and our retirement. I feel more than secure in the provision he has made for our family. "Lazy hands make a man poor, but diligent hands bring wealth" (Prov. 10:4).

I have no desire to raise sons who graduate college with no other goal than to sow their wild oats. The "provider" mentality should be at the forefront of their minds regardless of whether they have met their future bride. I hardly think it was God's plan for a vast number of Christian young men to postpone marriage and spend their postcollege years "gaming it up" with their buddies on the weekends, socking away their cash for big-screen TVs, and engaging in an occasional hook-up to satisfy their sexual urges. Trust me, there are plenty out there doing just that. Rest assured, I have encouraged my daughter to steer clear of such visionless "boys" who refuse to grow up. (Sorry, I can't bring myself to call them "men.")

A "Real" Man Is a Protector

If the *Titanic* were to sink today, only a little more than a third of the men would give up their spots on the lifeboats to women outside of their immediate families. This is according to

Pittsburgh *Post-Gazette*'s *"Titanic Test,"* where two hundred men were interviewed.[13] What ever happened to old-fashioned chivalry? The results of the *"Titanic* Test" should come as a relief to many feminists who have long scorned the preferential treatment gentlemen have historically extended to women in the name of good manners. On a recent flight, while I was wrestling to get my bag in the overhead bin, a nice gentleman came to the rescue. He kindly asked if he could help, and, of course, I welcomed his assistance. I thanked him for being one of a dying breed of gentlemen (just loud enough for the other male cads who had remained seated). He commented that he had been trained from an early age to be courteous and extend a hand to women in need. He shared that, at times, women have smirked at him for opening a door or offering his seat. I wonder if these same women would smirk at him if he were to offer them his seat on a lifeboat while on the deck of a sinking ship. Somehow I doubt it.

Chivalry is a word that sparks imagery of the Middle Ages and the days of wandering knights. It was a point of honor for knights to protect others, even at the cost of personal hardship, injury, or even death. Respect for women was an important part of the knight's code and formed a basis for many of the rules of politeness in our culture today. Unfortunately, those rules are not always followed.

At a recent visit to the orthodontist, my daughter and I walked in to find the waiting area full. We were about to take a seat on the floor when a man got up and signaled his two teenage sons to follow his lead and offer their seats to us. I thanked him profusely and overheard him talking to his sons about becoming more aware of situations when women are in need of a seat. It reminded me of our family trip to Disney World and a bus ride back to our hotel at the end of a long day.

We had been on our feet most of the day and were relieved finally to have the opportunity to sit for an extended period of time. After several stops, the bus had filled up, so my husband (being a gentleman) gave his seat to a woman who would otherwise have to stand in the middle aisle and hang on to a bar above her head. He nodded for my older son, Ryan, to do the same, and he quickly complied. (I made a note to check his forehead for fever.) Even so, there were not enough seats, and several children in the aisle were getting tossed about as they tried to hang onto their parents' legs. I was amazed at the number of young men who remained seated, fully aware of the circumstances. Finally, I stood up and offered a couple of small children my seat and told my daughter to do the same. She started to give me the "I'm a princess look" but thought better of it. I was teaching her that manners cross gender lines in the name of common courtesy.

There is no arguing that the single greatest influence in our sons' lives will be their fathers. Sons who witness fathers treating their mothers with respect will, most likely, grow up to be husbands who treat their wives with respect. I am fortunate to have a husband who models to our sons what it looks like to be a gentleman and a protector. He expects our sons to treat both my daughter and me with respect and courtesy. In addition, my boys have had the extra benefit of attending a Christian school (from kindergarten through eighth grade) where manners were taught and strictly enforced. Boys were expected to fall back in line and allow the girls to go first when walking down corridors. They were expected to hold the doors open for the girls and allow them to enter a room first.

Yet, in spite of my sons' training, they still have a tendency to forget their manners from time to time. Ryan used to forget his manners and walk ahead of me through doors, sometimes even failing to hold the door open. In order to nip this bad habit in the bud, I allowed the door to fold in on my body and waited. He finally turned around and rushed back (laughing) and opened the door. My stunt worked, and now he rushes to hold the door open for me, lest he risk public embarrassment. When in doubt, resort to public shaming!

In a 1948 issue of *Ladies' Home Journal* there is an advice column answered by none other than Eleanor Roosevelt. One young woman submitted this question: "Why is the reason men of the North seemingly show lack of respect for women? Men do not tip their hats to women whom they meet on the street, neither do they rise from their seats when women come into the room. Southern men are more courteous." Mrs. Roosevelt replied, "You surprise me in your estimate of men in the North. I have never had a man greet me in the street without raising his hat, nor do I find that they do not get up when a lady comes into the room."[14] Mrs. Roosevelt would roll over in her grave if she witnessed the lack of respect men display toward women today. It's probably a good thing she's not around to see the results of the "*Titanic* Test!"

A protector is humble in heart. He places the needs of others before his own. A husband who is a protector lives by Ephesians 5:25, which says, "Husbands, love your wives, just as Christ loved the church and gave himself up for her."

By the time my boys leave the nest, I hope and pray they will be polite young men who exhibit proper manners to women, extend a hand to those in need, and be the type to, literally, be willing to lay down their lives for women and children should they ever be faced with a real-life "*Titanic* Test."

Raising Your Son to Be a Spiritual Leader

What makes for a spiritual leader in today's world of Christian followers? If you want to raise a spiritual leader, check and see where your boy stands in regard to the five qualities of a godly man listed below.

1. A spiritual leader attends a Bible-believing church regularly. Consistent attendance in a Bible-believing church is essential for spiritual growth. Why is church attendance important? In a Bible-believing church, Christians learn the Bible and how to apply it to their lives, have an opportunity to fellowship with other believers, participate in corporate worship, and receive encouragement, accountability, and comfort.

When I was a Sunday school teacher years ago in the children's department, my heart was grieved over the children on my class roster who attended Sunday school and church only sporadically. While sporadic attendance was better than no attendance at all, moms' and/or dads' unwillingness to make Sunday school and church a priority sends the clear message to their children that Sunday school and church attendance is not a priority.

I was also grieved over the number of parents who told me they stopped attending Sunday school or church because one or more of their children did not want to go. Given that logic, I wonder if they let their children miss school on days they would rather sleep in or watch their favorite cartoon. The spiritual foundation established by consistent church attendance will lend itself to a stronger and deeper faith in Jesus.

2. A spiritual leader builds his life on a firm foundation. Many Christians treat their faith as an afterthought or merely one of many aspects that influence their lives, rather than being the preeminent, foundational aspect of their lives.

We can all probably think of times we were shocked when people have told us they are Christians, yet their lives did not support it. I can't help but think of Peter who denied Christ three times after declaring to him, "Even if all fall away, I will not" (Mark 14:29). Peter discovered the hard way that believing in Christ is not always easy. When his faith was tested, he chose safety over following Jesus. Peter faced a crisis of belief. Was this Jesus who he claimed to be? In the end Peter would determine that, indeed, Jesus was the Messiah, the Son of the living God. By the time he proclaimed Christ to thousands on the day of Pentecost, Peter had remolded his life to fit his faith. He was transformed from a closet Christian to one of the boldest and most vocal disciples of Christ ever known.

Would those who know you be shocked to discover that your son is a Christian? Would they be shocked to discover that you are a Christian? Would people identify your son as a faithful follower of Christ after spending time with him? Would they identify you as a faithful follower after spending time with you? These are painful questions to ask, but the truth is, if you have not built your own life on a firm foundation of faith, you will run the risk of modeling to your son a watered-down faith. If this is the case, he may conclude that "Christian" is merely a label that one wears rather than a way of life. The only way to prevent this is to develop your life on your faith in Jesus rather than attempt to make your faith fit comfortably into your life. By modeling this to your son, it will remove any doubt that Christianity is a way of life rather than a label in life.

3. A spiritual leader tithes. A recent Barna Research survey found that only 6 percent of born-again Christian households tithed to their churches in 2002.[15] Malachi 3:10 instructs us to "'Bring the whole tithe into the storehouse, that there may be food in my house. Test me in this,' says the LORD Almighty, 'and see if I will not throw open the floodgates of heaven and pour out so much blessing that you will not have room enough for it.'" A tithe is defined as 10 percent of our earnings. In giving a tenth of our income back to God, we acknowledge that 100 percent of all we have belongs to God, and without him we would have nothing.

Why is tithing a characteristic of spiritual leadership? If one claims to believe wholeheartedly in Christ and the commandments set forth in God's Word, he/she should be willing to entrust to God a portion (10 percent or more) of what belongs to him in the first place. Regardless of whether a Christian's failure to tithe is due to a real or perceived lack of finances or simply a preference to spend the money elsewhere, failure to tithe shows a lack of trust in God. If we cannot trust God with our finances, we will struggle to trust him in other areas of life, as well.

Who can forget the widow's gift of two copper coins that caught the eye of Jesus? He noted that while the others gave their gifts out of their wealth, the widow gave out of her poverty. It is not the amount of one's gift that matters to God but the act of obedience in giving, one's attitude in giving, and the level of sacrifice.

As mothers, we must model the discipline of tithing to our children and train them to tithe their allowance and other income they earn. Children who grow up tithing 10 percent of their earnings are much more likely to tithe in their adult years. I have told my daughter that she should not even consider marrying a man who compromises in the area of tithing. In doing so, such a man shows a lack of faith in God that will not be limited to his finances. If he can dismiss God's command to tithe when it becomes difficult to do so, what keeps him from dismissing the command to remain faithful in marriage whenever the marriage gets difficult?

God's command in Malachi to bring our tithes to the storehouse is preceded by a reprimand that the people were robbing God of his tithes. Our children must be taught that in addition to demonstrating a lack of faith in God, one's decision not to tithe is a decision to rob God of what belongs to him.

When my husband and I were newly married and in the market for a new home, we met with a real estate agent. We were not sure of the price range of houses we could afford, so the agent assisted us in calculating what price of home we could qualify to purchase based on our salary and monthly expenses. When my husband got to the amount we paid monthly in a tithe to our church, she was stunned and asked if it was negotiable. She explained that we could afford a much nicer home if we were willing to give up the tithe amount and put it toward the house payment. We walked out of her office and never looked back. What a shame that she did not realize that we would be far more blessed in giving our tithe to God than living in a home with a few hundred more square feet.

I am so grateful to be married to a spiritual leader who, when his faith is tested, puts his money where his mouth is. I pray my sons will also display this critical quality of spiritual leadership. Christians who are not in the habit of tithing disqualify themselves from being called spiritual leaders.

4. A spiritual leader refers regularly to God's instruction manual for living. In the December 1948 *Ladies' Home Journal*, the following ad for Oxford Bibles can be found: "This Christmas . . . give your child the Bible. A fine Bible is the rightful inheritance of every young American. As the Pilgrims drew from it their dream that this nation might be founded in freedom . . . and Roosevelt his dream of the Four Freedoms for all the nations of the world . . . so from its pages today's young leaders will build tomorrow."[16]

In our culture today the Bible is rarely acknowledged and, when it is, it is often referred to as a man-made compilation of stories and spiritual insights or opinions. As mothers, we must be active in teaching our sons that the Bible is no ordinary book. The Bible is God's revelation of himself to mankind. It contains his words, truths, standards, and principles. It reveals his character and presents his message of love and redemption.

Second Timothy 3:16–17 says: "All Scripture is God-breathed and is useful for teaching, rebuking, correcting and training in righteousness, so that the man of God may be thoroughly equipped for every good work." God inspired more than forty authors to write the Bible over a span of fifteen hundred years. It was written in three languages, in thirteen countries, covering three continents. Nevertheless, it has unity of message.

Does your son recognize that the Bible is his instruction manual for living? Do you model to him a dependence on God's Word? Spiritual leaders do not rely on man's wisdom to get through life. They filter everything life throws their way through God's Word. A spiritual leader will initiate time spent in God's

Word and do so on a consistent basis. "Your statutes are my heritage forever; they are the joy of my heart" (Ps. 119:111).

5. A spiritual leader prays without ceasing. When I was a
new believer, I remember experiencing some confusion over the
call in 1 Thessalonians 5:17 to "pray without ceasing" (KJV).
How does one pray constantly? The Greek word used for "without ceasing" is *adialeiptos,* which means "uninterruptedly." Since
prayer is the way we communicate with God, and communicating with God is critical to living our lives in accordance to God's
will, it only makes sense that we should be mindful of anything
that would interrupt our communication with God. While I
believe it is important to have a set time for prayer, it does not
have to be relegated only to that time. We must teach our sons
that God is accessible every minute of every day. When they
develop the instinct to turn to God throughout their day,
whether to lift up a request or a praise to him, they will learn
the art of what it is to pray without ceasing. Boys who develop
the habit of taking thought of and talking to God throughout
each day on their own initiative are much less likely to fall into
tempting situations or make foolish decisions when standing at
the crossroads of a difficult choice.

Prayer, simply put, is conversing with God. The more our
sons converse with God, the more in touch they will be with his
intended purpose for their lives. A consistent prayer life can act
as a safeguard against mediocrity and a tendency toward a luke-
warm Christian faith. Well-balanced conversations with God
include both talking to God and listening to him. After all, how
good would a relationship with a friend be if our conversations
always boiled down to a long to-do list for the other person.

Philippians 4:6 says, "By prayer and petition, with thanks-
giving, present your requests to God." There is certainly nothing
wrong with asking God to do things for us, but there are other
aspects of prayer that are also important. One of the simplest
and best prayer models I have found that leads to a well-balanced prayer life is the ACTS model. ACTS is an acronym that

stands for adoration (or praise), confession, thanks, and supplication (making requests of God for others and ourselves). My husband and I use the ACTS model of prayer, and we have diligently taught it to our children and used it as part of their bedtime ritual when they were young. Because of this, they are comfortable praying aloud, not to mention leading others in prayer. I have married friends who are heartsick that they have never heard their husbands pray out loud. The ability to lead others in prayer is a requirement for a spiritual leader. Most importantly, I want my boys to know that God is only a prayer away and to be in the habit of taking matters to his throne of grace.

As mothers, we have been given a tremendous calling to raise the next generation of godly men. We have our work cut out for us, but it is important to remember that we do not labor alone. Our sons will be our boys forever, but they are, above all, God's son. In the meantime, enjoy your boys. Savor each and every moment you have with them. Spend time with them. Talk to them. Laugh with them. And rejoice in their each and every milestone as they journey the road to manhood.

If your boys are young, take heed from a mom who will soon drop her boy off at college—it goes by so very fast. I recently read the introduction of this book to my older son, Ryan. Several times I had to stop and choke back tears as I reflected back on his earlier days. He chuckled when I read the following:

> I will stumble upon a reminder of the days gone past and quickly be reduced to tears. . . . A picture of a bashful preschooler on his first day of school proudly holding his new Ninja Turtle lunchbox. A home movie where he is jumping off the couch wearing nothing more than his homemade Batman cape and white briefs. A tattered and worn copy of his favorite book

Go Dog Go! I read it so many times I had it memorized. What I would give to read it just one more time.

When I finished reading him the introduction, he put his arm around me and said, "Mom, before I leave for college, you can read me *Go Dog Go!* one more time." I plan to take him up on that.

> *Heavenly Father, we ask you to come alongside*
> *us as we labor to raise our boys to be godly men.*
> *Only by your power and mercy can we face*
> *the challenges that lie ahead. Help us to enjoy these*
> *precious and fleeting years. Above all, thank you*
> *for trusting us for a time . . . with your boys.*

Acknowledgments

Were it not for the support of my family, I could not do what I do. I have said it before in my acknowledgments, but it bears repeating. When God called me into the ministry of writing and speaking, he called my entire family.

Keith, you amaze me. You are the one who should be writing books. You have faithfully modeled commitment to family, servant leadership in the church, and most importantly, devotion to God. Thank you for being my husband, editor, advisor, counselor, and most of all, best friend. Our sons are blessed to have a father who has modeled what it is to be a godly man.

Paigey, you are the daughter every mom dreams of having. Thank you for not just supporting what I do, but being a part of it.

Hayden, my tender warrior. You and your brother have inspired so much of what I write about in this book. Thank you for allowing me to share the stories. I promise to always ask first.

Ryan, pass me a tissue please. I can't believe mama's boy is off to college. I can't stand to think about how quiet it will be when you leave. I will miss you terribly, but I am so excited for this new chapter in your life. And, by the way, for the next four years I am giving priority to all speaking invitations within a hundred mile radius of Auburn, Alabama! War Eagle!

To the Virtuous Reality staff: Thank you for your never-ending support. You make it possible for me to stick to my calling. You are each gifted in areas where I am not and it brings a peace to know that the ministry runs smoothly in my absence. Susan, thank you for sourcing the footnotes in the back of this book! Have I mentioned how much I hate sourcing footnotes?

To Susie Davis, thank you for your friendship, wisdom, and occasional shoulder to cry on. Congrats on that new book of yours!

To Jackie Kendall, Lisa Ryan, and Jami Smith: It has been a joy to share the platform with each of you. You are amazing women of God.

To Bill Jensen, my fun friend in the sometimes, wacky world of Christian publishing: thank you for cheering me on. You make me laugh.

To my wonderful friends at B&H and LifeWay. Thank you for your willingness to partner with me in this calling. To Len Goss, let the record state that my dog is better than your dog. Lexie Grace sends her love.

To Lee Hough, Literary Agent Extraordinaire: Thanks for taking care of the fine print and details, so I can stick to writing. I am so grateful that God allowed our paths to cross.

Most of all, to my Lord and Savior, Jesus Christ: Apart from you, I am nothing. I am fully aware that you don't need me to accomplish your kingdom purposes. I stand in amazement that you would pick me to play any part at all in bringing glory to your name.

Notes

Chapter 3: A Mother's Sphere of Influence

1. Henry G. Bosch, "Godly Mothers," *The Daily Bread*, May 8, Bible.org, accessed June 1, 2005, www.bible.org/illus.asp?topic_id=1771.

2. David and Teresa Ferguson, Paul and Vicky Warren, and Terri Ferguson, *Parenting with Intimacy* (Colorado Springs, CO: Victor Books, 1995).

3. The Barna Group, *Americans Speak: Enron, WorldCom and Others Are Result of Inadequate Moral Training by Families*, www.barna.org, accessed June 30, 2005, www.barna.org/FlexPage.aspx?Page=BarnaUpdate&BarnaUpdateID=117.

4. George Gallup Jr. and Timothy Jones, *The Next American Spirituality* (Colorado Springs, CO: Chariot Victor Publishing, 2000).

5. The Barna Group, *Americans Speak: Enron, WorldCom and Others Are Result of Inadequate Moral Training by Families*, www.barna.org, accessed June 30, 2005, www.barna.org/FlexPage.aspx?Page=BarnaUpdate&BarnaUpdateID=117.

6. George Barna, *Real Teens* (Ventura, CA: Regal Books, 2001).

7. Ibid.

Chapter 6: Searching for Worth in All the Wrong Places

1. Diane Carlson Jones, Thorbjorg Helga Vigfusdottir, and Yoonsun Lee, "Body Image and the Appearance Culture Among Adolescent Girls and Boys: An Examination of Friend Conversations, Peer Criticism, Appearance Magazines, and the Internalization of Appearance Idols," Journal of Adolescent Research, May 2004; vol. 19: no. 3, 323–39.

2. J. K. Thompson, L. J. Heinberg, M. Altabe, and S. Tantleff-Dunn, "Exacting beauty: Theory, assessment, and treatment of body image disturbances" (Washington, D.C.: American Psychological Association, 1999).

3. M. Rauste-von Wright, "Body image satisfaction in adolescent boys and girls: A longitudinal study," *Journal of Youth and Adolescence*, 1989.

4. G. H. Cohane and H. G. Pope Jr., "Body image in boys: A review of the literature," *International Journal of Eating Disorders*, 2001.

Chapter 7: Babylon: Will Your Boy Bow Down?

1. Misty Bernall, *She Said Yes* (Farmington, PA: Plough Publishing House, 1999).

2. George Barna, *Real Teens* (Ventura, CA: Regal Books, 2001).

3. Josh McDowell, *Beyond Belief to Conviction* (Carol Stream, IL: Tyndale House Publishers, 2002).

4. Dan Smithwick, "One Generation to Go, Then the End," *Nehemiah Institute*, February 2002, www.nehemiahinstitute.com, accessed June 15, 2005, www.nehemiahinstitute.com/articles/index.php?action=show&id=18.

5. *Biblesoft's New Exhaustive Strong's Numbers and Concordance with Expanded Greek-Hebrew Dictionary*, Copyright (c) 1994, Biblesoft and International Bible Translators, Inc.

Chapter 8: Surviving a Sex-Obsessed Culture

1. See www.50centonline.com/massacre07.php, Artist: 50 Cent, Album: The Massacre, Song: *Candy Shop*, accessed August 5, 2005.

2. "Sexuality, Contraception, and the Media, American Academy of Pediatrics Committee on Public Education," January 2001 www.aap.org/policcy/re0038.html.

3. See http://money.cnn.com/2005/01/05/technology/personaltech/playboy_ipod/, "Playboy Coming to iPod' Magazine to offer photo galleries that can be viewed on digital media players, including iPod.," 5 January 2005, accessed June 23, 2005.

4. Molly Wood, "Warning: adult content . . . everywhere"; http://www.cnet.com/4520-6033_1-6128680-1.html, CNET.com, 5 April 2005, accessed March 15, 2005.

5. See www.beverlylahayeinstitute.org, 2003.

6. Kaiser Family Foundation, "Generation M: Media in the Lives of 8–18 Year-olds," 8 March 2005, www.kff.org.

7. Brent Bozell, "MTV knows no shame," www.townhall.com/columnists/brentbozell/bb20050206.shtml; accessed February 6, 2005.

8. Ibid.

9. Ibid.

10. Ibid.

11. National Institute on Media and the Family, Fact Sheet MTV,

www.mediafamily.org/facts/facts_mtv.shtml, accessed June 29, 2005; secondary source: Parents Television Council, MTV's Defense of Its Offensive Language is Offensive, www.parentstv.org/ptc/campaigns/ MTV/main.asp, accessed June 29, 2005.

12. Benoit Denizet-Lewis, "Friends, Friends with Benefits and the Benefits of the Local Mall," *The New York Times Magazine*, 30 May 2004.

13. Ibid.

14. Karen S. Peterson, "Younger kids trying it now, often ignorant of disease risks," *USA Today*, 16 November 2000, D1.

15. The Guttmacher Report, August 2001, www.guttmacher.org/ pubs/tgr/04/4/index.html, accessed July 2, 2005.

16. "Sex/Not Sex: For many teens, oral doesn't count," *USA Today*, 16 November 2000, D1.

17. Ibid.

18. U.S. Centers for Disease Control and Prevention, "2001 Youth Risk Behavior Survey," www.cdc.gov/mmwr/preview/mmwrhtml/ ss504al.htm, accessed July 1, 2005.

19. Ibid.

20. CBSnews.com; "Taking the Pledge," 22 May 2005. www.cbs news.com/stories/2005/05/20/60minutes/main696975_page2.shtm.

21. "Abstinence Statistics and Studies: Teen Virginity Pledges Lead to Better Life Outcomes, Study Finds," The Heritage Foundation POSTED, date accessed 21 September 2004; www.abstinence.net/ library/index.php?entryid=1396.

22. Ibid.

23.Neil Howe and William Strauss, *Millennials Rising: The Next Great Generation* (Vintage Publishers, 2000).

24. Recent findings from The "Add Health" Survey: Teens and Sexual Activity, Alan Guttmacher Institute, www.guttmacher.org/ pubs/tgr/04/4/gr040401.html, accessed June 1, 2005.

25. "With One Voice: America's Adults and Teens Sound Off about Teen Pregnancy," The National Campaign to Prevent Teen Pregnancy, www.teenpregnancy.org/resources/data/pdf/WOV2004.pdf, accessed June 1, 2005.

26. Ibid.

27. Ibid. Two-thirds of all sexually experienced teens (63 percent of boys and 69 percent of girls) said they wish they had waited longer to have sex.

28. *Seventeen*, January 2003, 115.

29. "United States Birth Rates for Teens, 15–19," National Campaign to Prevent Teen Pregnancy, www.teenpregnancy.org/resources/data/ brates.asp, accessed June 2005.

30. Jeff Sharlet, "The Young and the Sexless," *Rolling Stone*, June 2005, www.rollingstone.com/news/story/_/id/7418688.

Chapter 9: Staying in Line When Online

1. Amanda Lenhart, "Protecting Teens Online," Washington, D.C.: Pew Internet & American Life Project, 16 March 2005, www.pewinternet.org/PPF/r/152/report_display.asp.

2. Crimes Against Children Research Center's Youth Internet Safety Survey, www.unh.edu/ccrc/youth_interest_safety_survey.html, accessed June 25, 2005.

3. Anne Collier, US kids' media use: major study, www.netfamilynews.org/nl050311.html, accessed March 25, 2005.

4. "Teens and Online Marketing," 10 October 2003, www.webadvantage.net/tip_archive.cfm?tip_id=293&&a=1.

5. E'blaster program, www.spectorsoft.com, accessed June 25, 2005.

6. Kimberly J. Mitchell, Ph.D., David Finkelhor, Ph.D., and Janis Wolak, J.D., "Risk Factors for and Impact of Online Sexual Solicitation of Youth," *The Journal of the American Medical Association*, vol. 285, no. 23; 20 June 2001.

7. Brad Wright of CNN, "Sounding the alarm on video game ratings," http://archives.cnn.com/2002/TECH/fun.games/12/19/games.ratings/index.html, accessed March 15, 2005.

8. Lawrence Journal World; LJWorld.com; "Gaming addiction growing;" 4 June 2005;www2.ljworld.com/news/2005/jun/04/game_addiction.

9. Jennifer Emily, "Predators reading teen blogs, too; Some schools ban access to Web sites," 4 May 2005, *The Dallas Morning News*; www.dallasnews.com/sharedcontent/dws/dn/latestnews/stories/050405dnccoxanga.72f2653a.html.

10. SafeKids Net Family News, www.netfamilynews.org. (I highly recommend that parents sign up for this free online newsletter!)

11. Ibid.

12. London School of Economics, January 2002, www.protectkids.com/dangers/stats.htm#youth, accessed August 1, 2005.

13. Family Safe Media, www.nscn.org/article.asp?iArticleID=128, accessed August 2, 2005.

14. Kaiser Family Foundation, www.nscn.org/article.asp?iArticleID=128, accessed July 2, 2005.

15. Bella English, "The Secret Life of Boys," 12 May 2005, the *Boston Globe*, www.boston.com/news/globe/living/articles/2005/05/12/the_secret_life_of_boys?pg=full.

16. Stephen Arterburn, Fred Stoeker, and Mike Yorkey, *Every Young Man's Battle* (Colorado Springs, CO: WaterBrook Press, 2002).

17. National Center for Missing and Exploited Children and Cox Communications, www.missingkids.org, accessed August 2, 2005.

18. Ibid.

19. See www.crosswalk.com, The Al Mohler Crosswalk Commentary: "Pornified America—The Culture of Pornography," 22 August 2005; reference is to Pamela Paul, author of *Pornified: How Pornography Is Transforming Our Live1s, Our Relationships, and Our Families* (Time Books, 2005).

Chapter 11: Manhood, Masculinity, and Marriage Redefined

1. *Seventeen*, April 1960.

2. Heirloom Sterling, *Seventeen*, May 1960, 75.

3. Towle Silversmiths, *Seventeen*, April 1960, 9.

4. *Seventeen*, August 1972; September, November, April, July 1973; August 1974.

5. Gloria Steinem quote (second hand reports), http://archive. salon.com/mwt/feature/1998/03/27feature.html.

6. Judith Hennessee, *Betty Friedan: Her Life* (New York: Random House, 1999).

7. *Cosmogirl.*

8. "Women Warned of Infertility Trap," 11 April 2002, www.CNN. com/Health.

9. See www.davidandgoliathtees.com/index.php?mode=B, accessed August 6, 2005.

10. Christina Hoff Sommers, *The War against Boys: How Misguided Feminism Is Harming Our Young Men* (New York, NY: Simon & Schuster, 2000).

11. Ibid.

12. Ibid.

13. Doug Giles, "Metrosexual or Medieval," www.townhall.com/ columnists/douggiles/dg20050416.shtml, accessed April 16, 2005.

14. Ibid.

15. "Estimated Age at First Marriage," U.S. Census Bureau, 2000; age data from the U. S. Bureau of the Census, *Current Population Reports*, 2000, www.census.gov/population/www/socdemo/hhfam ily.html, accessed July 24, 2005.

16. Albert Mohler, "What If There Are No Adults?" 19 August 2005, http://www.crosswalk.com/news/weblogs/mohler/?ad ate=8/19/2005#1346589.

17. Ibid.

18. Ibid.

19. David Papanoe, "Why men are slow to marry," http://she knows.com/about/look/1451.htm, accessed August 19, 2005.

20. "Hooking Up, Hanging Out and Hoping for Mr. Right: College Women on Mating and Dating Today," Independent Women's Forum; The Hook-up Study (July 2001) www.americanvalues.org/html/apr_ hooking_up.html, accessed August 10, 2005.

21. Kathleen Parker, "In Matters of Sex, Things Never Change," *Orlando Sentinel*.

22. Larry Bumpass and Hsien-Hen Lu, "Trends in Cohabitation and Implications for Children's Family Contexts in the US," *Population Studies* 54 (2000), 29–41.

23. US Census Current Population Survey (2004) www.usatoday. com/life/lifestyle/2005-07-17-cohabitation_x.htm, accessed July 17, 2005.

24. The study is featured in the National Marriage Project's annual report on the social health of marriage in America, "The State of Our Unions: 2002." Study findings were based on eight focus groups with sixty not-yet-married heterosexual men, ages twenty-five to thirty-three. Focus groups were conducted January 2002 to April 2002 in four major metropolitan areas: northern New Jersey, Chicago, Washington D.C., and Houston.

25. "Snapshots," *USA Today*, 10 June 2003, D1.

26. National Marriage Project, http://marriage.rutgers.edu, accessed August 1, 2005.

27. Ibid.

28. Ibid.

29. Frederica Mathewes-Green, "First Things," August/September 2005, www.firstthings.com cited by Albert Mohler, "What If There Are No Adults?" 19 August 2005, www.crosswalk.com/news/weblogs/ mohler/?adate=8/19/2005#1346589.

30. Ibid.

31. Rose Kreider and Jason Fields, "Number, Timing, and Duration of Marriages and Divorces: 1996," *Current Population Reports* (2002), www.census.gov/prod/2002pubs/p70-80.pdf, accessed July 25, 2005.

32. "Hooking Up, Hanging Out and Hoping for Mr. Right: College Women on Mating and Dating Today," Independent Women's Forum; The Hook-up Study (July 2001) www.americanvalues.org/html/apr_ hooking_up.html, accessed July 20, 2005.

33. "Cohabitation Is Replacing Dating," www.usatoday.com/life/ lifestyle/2005-07-17-cohabitation_x.htm.

34. Larry Bumpass and Hsien-Hen Lu, "Trends in Cohabitation and Implications for Children's Family Contexts in the United States," *Population Studies*, (2002), 54:29–41.

35. Tom Smith, "The Emerging 21st Century Family" (National Opinion Research Center, University of Chicago, 1999).

36. George Barna Report, www.barna.org/FlexPage.aspx?Page=BarnaUpdate&BarnaUpdateID=170, accessed August 3, 2005.

37. George Barna Report, www.barna.org/FlexPage.aspx?Page=BarnaUpdate&BarnaUpdateID=170, accessed August 3, 2005.

38. US Census Report, 2000.

39. Ibid.

40. National Center for Health Statistics, 2000 data, reported in 2002.

41. US Census Bureau, 2000.

42. The National Marriage Project, 2004.

43. "Men raised in traditional family households are more likely to marry." *Men's Health News*, www.News-Medical.Net, 25 June 2004, www.news-medical.net/?id=2810 http://www.rutgers.edu.

Chapter 13: Raising Your Boy to Be a Real Man

1. Nicole Beland, "Babes in Boyland," *Men's Health*, October 2004.

2. Ibid.

3. Ibid.

4. Ibid.

5. Ibid.

6. Ibid.

7. Rutgers National Marriage Project 2001, http://marriage.rutgers.edu/Publications/SOOU/NMPAR2001.pdf, accessed August 2, 2005.

8. Nicole Beland, "Babes in Boyland," *Men's Health*, October 2004.

9. Shaunti Feldhahn, *For Women Only: What You Need to Know about the Inner Lives of Men* (Sisters, OR: Multnomah, 2004).

10. Ibid.

11. Ibid.

12. Albert Mohler, "What If There Are No Adults?" 19 August 2005, www.crosswalk.com/news/weblogs/mohler/?adate=8/19/2005#1346589.

13. Rochester *Democrat and Chronicle*, 14 April 1992. Pittsburgh (AP).

14. *Ladies' Home Journal*, December 1948.

15. George Barna, "Americans Donate Billions to Charity, but Giving to Churches has Declined, April 2005, www.barna.org/

FlexPage.aspx?Page=BarnaUpdate&BarnaUpdateID=1, accessed July 1, 2005.

16. *Ladies' Home Journal*, December 1948, 185.

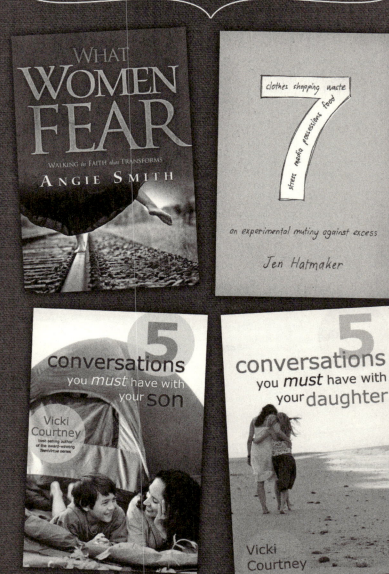